"All the World's a Stage…"
Know Your Chart…You'll Know Your Part!

This Self-Discovery Workbook Belongs to

_____

My BIRTH INFORMATION:

DATE of BIRTH _____
TIME of BIRTH _____AM_____PM
PLACE of BIRTH _____
                CITY   STATE   COUNTRY

Introduction

William Shakespeare once said "All the world is a stage, and we are like the poor player who struts and frets his hour upon the stage and then is heard no more." In a play, the actor is not always on stage. He or she is either preparing for their part, changing costumes, or just waiting to return to the stage. At the end of the play, he or she takes a bow and then waits for the revues!

How does this apply to the ancient, symbolic language of Astrology? Your CHART, which is based upon the exact TIME, DATE & PLACE of your BIRTH, is your SCRIPT! Your SCRIPT shows the many PARTS you are capable of playing on the great stage of life. If you are like most of us, there seems to be many sides to what is called your personality, and even, at times, many "selves" within your self! Your personality expresses itself in the many ROLES you play in life.

The teen years, and early twenties, are ones of discovery, making new friends and all about acquiring skills which will help us throughout our lives. This workbook is designed for the TEEN or YOUNG ADULT who is beginning the quest for self-understanding. This workbook will take you step-by-step, into the process an Astrologer uses when he or she interprets your CHART/ SCRIPT. You too will be able to read (and understand) your own SCRIPT, in order to be able to better time your ENTRANCES & EXITS on the stage of life, as you play your many ROLES.

In order to use this workbook, you will need to have your Natal Astrology chart already prepared. There is an **order form** in the back of this book if you don't already have a chart. **Other materials** you will need for this workbook will be **a pencil, colored pencils, pens or markers.**

Table of Contents

Chapter 1

What is an Astrology Chart?

Your Astrology Chart or "STAR MAP" is your blueprint for being and shows the many CYCLES of expression that you will experience on this EARTH SCHOOL planet. Understanding your Astrology chart is a most effective way to "conscious awareness" and engages that part of you that already knows everything. It is very revealing, empowering, quite exciting...and a lot of FUN!

Astrology or "map of the stars", originally was named the "Zodiac", from the Greek 'zodiakos", meaning 'circle of animals'...a band in the heavens divided into twelve Signs, each containing 30 degrees of longitude and acting as the barometer for various human traits. The Greeks believed in mythology, which gave god-like qualities to human expression. The myths were stories that created a way of understanding the human condition.

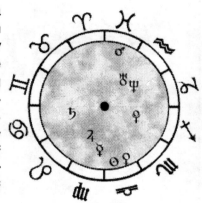

Your birth chart, or horoscope, is represented in the form of a wheel, and is a diagram of the sky at a particular moment in time...your birth time. The symbols ("glyphs") represent the many different modes of expression possible and the movement of the planets expresses the cycles that are experienced by all living things. Each of these astrological factors are symbolic of the language many humans express in their sub-conscious. These expressions may be activated and brought to your awareness by circumstances in your life, which then present you with a range of choices. Your choices can be limited and determined by your character, which is itself revealed through an understanding of the symbols that make up the chart.

Everything is energy. We are electromagnetic, MULTI-DIMENSIONAL, spiritual beings inhabiting a physical body. Your personal STAR MAP™ or Astrology Chart shows where the planets were placed in the heavens at the exact hour of your birth. The PLANETS in a chart represent certain ENERGIES, the SIGN those PLANETS are in, show HOW the ENERGY is used, and the HOUSES the PLANETS fall in, show WHERE, or in what area of your life you will USE those energies.

Interpretation of your chart is based upon analyzing age-old, archetypal mythological symbols for the human condition. No one's chart is all "good" or all "bad". One can use the energies in a mature or immature way. "Difficult" aspects can represent challenges, as well as strengths a person might have, while "easy" aspects can represent certain talents you were born with.

Here is how one of my clients described her experience with Astrology:

"I was truly amazed. It felt as if I had stepped into my soul! I was learning things I already knew about myself...but didn't know that I knew! Astrology helped me to see me as the unique person that I am and all that I can be." Sherilyn

May your journey into Self-Discovery be a Cosmic one! *Kathleen Scott* C.A.P.

The Signs of the Zodiac

March 20 - April 20

April 21 - May 20

May 21 - June 21

June 22 - July 22

July 23 - August 23

August 24 - September 22

September 23 - October 23

October 24 - November 22

November 23 - December

December 22 - January 21

January 20 - February 18

February 19 - March 20

The Planets & Their Symbols

SUN

MOON

MERCURY

VENUS

MARS

JUPITER

SATURN

URANUS

NEPTUNE

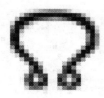

NORTH NODE

PLUTO

SOUTH NODE

Draw the
CORRECT SYMBOLS
for each Planet

SUN

MOON

MERCURY

VENUS

MARS

JUPITER

SATURN

URANUS

NEPTUNE

NORTH NODE

PLUTO

SOUTH NODE

The PLANETS

"WHAT" the ENERGIES are!

 The SUN: Power urge, conscious will, ego, vitalizing & life-giving force, ambition & pride. Symbol of masculinity & self-assertiveness.

 The MOON: Submissive, domestic urge, emotions, instincts, the subconscious, disposition, sensitivity & adaptability, symbol of femininity & receptivity, mother, home.

 MERCURY: Intellectual urge, conscious reasoning mind, communication, self-expression, judgment & dexterity. Symbol of mentality, ideas & interests.

 VENUS: Social urge, balancing, harmonizing, peace-making influence, attractiveness, cooperativeness, responsiveness, art, music, pleasurable activities, symbol of friendship, affection & artistry.

 MARS: Initiative, sexual and aggressive urge, combativeness, dynamic energy, impulsiveness, enterprise & physical courage.

 JUPITER: Good Luck, expansion urge, wisdom, protectiveness, generosity, idealism & aspirations. Symbol of opportunity, faith, confidence, optimism & tolerance.

 SATURN: Security urge, responsibility, self-discipline, endurance, patience, caution & stability. Symbol of authority, duty, seriousness & dependability.

 URANUS: Freedom urge, individualism, inventiveness, originality, erratic action & surprises. Symbol of awakening, evolution, change, rebellion & unpredictability.

 NEPTUNE: Spiritual or escape urge, impressionability, imagination, compassion & self-deception. Symbol of renewal, transformation & new beginnings

 PLUTO: Reforming urge, rebirth, regeneration, obsession to destroy the old & to create the new. Symbol of transformation, renewal & new beginnings.

☊ **NORTH NODE:** Symbolizes the path of personal integration through which there can be fulfillment & emotional growth & satisfaction.

☋ **SOUTH NODE**: Symbolizes the path of least resistance, the habit patterns of the past that should be outgrown or discarded and is always opposite the NORTH NODE.

"HOW" the ENERGIES operate!
The SIGNS, SYMBOLS & their Planetary RULERS

ARIES: (March 20-April 20) Ruled by the Planet MARS. Cardinal/ Fire, Symbol: The Ram. Individualistic, independent, self-reliant, courageous, enthusiastic, impulsive, assertive, impatient, intense, passionate, creative, turbulent, self-centered, natural pioneers, strong desire to be at the head of things, always into new projects.

TAURUS: (April 21– May 20) Ruled by the Planet VENUS. Fixed/ Earth, Symbol: The Bull. Domestic, patient, persistent, gentle & affectionate. Much concern with emotional and financial security, sensuous, self-indulgent, down-to-earth, conservative, loyal and possessive, practical, reliable, powerful endurance, attached to home & family.

GEMINI: (May 21—June 21) Ruled by the Planet MERCURY. Mutable/Air, Symbol: The Twins. Airy, intellectual, curious, versatile, quick, clever, active, love of variety, restless. Great capacity for observation, imitation & communication, youthful, non-combative, talkative, witty, tendency to scatter energies & ideas.

CANCER: (June 22, July 23) Ruled by the MOON Cardinal/Water, Symbol: The Crab. Sensitive, receptive, emotional, active imagination, well-developed instincts, heartfelt, strong feelings; greatly influenced by environment, tendency towards moodiness & insecurity, tenacious, strong sense of value & economy, nurturing & protective of loved ones. Can be emotional blackmailers.

LEO: (July 23—August 22) Ruled by the SUN Fixed/Fire, Symbol: The Lion. Generous, loyal, faithful, affectionate, proud, dignified, luxury-loving, confident, warm open & honest, dramatic, ardent, strong-willed, love to be the center of attention, persistent, cheerful, sunny, sociable, pleasure-oriented, good leaders.

VIRGO: (August 23—September 23) Ruled by the Planet MERCURY. Mutable/Earth, Symbol: The Virgin. Industrious, reserved, fastidious, analytical, critical, studious, Their work is the hub of their universe. Need to help others help themselves, sympathetic, service-oriented, good with details, discriminating, practical, tendency to worry too much, perfectionists.

"HOW" the ENERGIES operate!
The SIGNS, SYMBOLS & their Planetary RULERS

 LIBRA: (September 24—October 23) Ruled by the planet VENUS. Cardinal/Air Symbol: The Scales. Gentle, courteous, kind, refined, strong desire for peace & harmony, friendship & relationship very important, eager to please, friendly, charming, artistic, cooperative, active social nature, needs mental stimulation with others, appreciative of the arts.

 **SCORPIO:** (October 22—November 22) Ruled by the planet PLUTO Fixed/Water. Symbol: The Scorpio, the Eagle. Strong emotional desires, brave, courageous, strong-willed, persistent and enduring, warrior of the zodiac, will fight to protect loved ones, reserved, secretive, penetrating mind, strong likes & dislikes, sexual, forceful character, executive abilities.

 **SAGITTARIUS:** (November 23—December 21) Ruled by the planet JUPITER. Mutable/Fire Symbol: The Archer upon a Horse. Worldly, optimistic, philosophical, prophetic, outgoing, honest, direct, open-minded, generous, honorable, religious, love of freedom, independent, & the far horizons, ability to cultivate the mind in higher learning or through travel, highly restless.

 **CAPRICORN:** (December 22—January 20) Ruled by the planet SATURN. Cardinal/Earth. Symbol: The Goat. Trustworthy, responsible, patient, conservative, cautious, economical, thrifty, must watch tendency to self-denial, fatalism, must learn through experience, strong feelings of duty, earthy, ambitious, practical, acquisitive, authority-oriented, hard-working. Strong desire to "get ahead".

 **AQUARIUS:** (January 20—February 18) Ruled by the planet URANUS. Fixed/Air. Symbol: Man pouring water. Inventive, intellectual, fond of literature & science, tolerant, reasonable, oriented to partnership & companionship, great humanitarians, independent, fixed in their opinions, strong-willed, clear & logical in their thinking processes, They are a "mirror" for others.

 **PISCES:** (February 19—March 19) Ruled by the planet NEPTUNE. Mutable/Water Symbol: Two Fish. Impressionable, mystical, intuitive, deeply compassionate, adaptable, idealistic & sensitive. Tendency to day-dream, sympathetic & understanding of the underdog, feelings are easily aroused, active imagination, love to help others, but often get used.

The 12 NATURAL HOUSES of the CHART
"WHERE" the Energies Operate

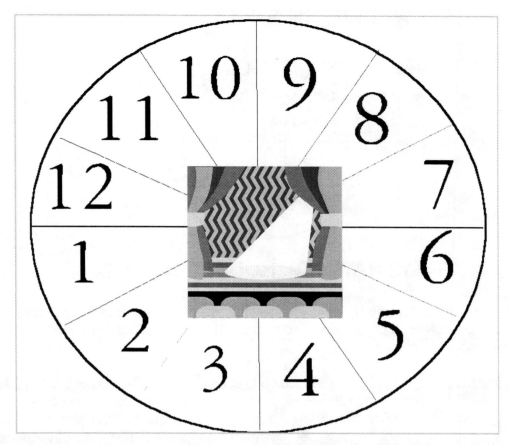

**The Natural HOUSES: The STAGE WHERE the ENERGIES are operating
The SIGNS of the ZODIAC & The PLANETS that Rule those HOUSES.**

1. **ARIES** (Ruled by Mars): Self-awareness, personality, physical body, the head, personal power.
2. **TAURUS** (Ruled by Venus): Self-worth, income, possessions, emotional needs, personal resources & talents.
3. **GEMINI** (Ruled by Mercury): Mental activity, short trips, communication, classes, brothers & sisters & neighbors.
4. **CANCER** (Ruled by the Moon): Home & family interests, property, security, roots, end of life, base of operation, the Mother.
5. **LEO** (Ruled by the Sun): Creativity, children, new projects, love affairs, fun & pleasure, speculation, gambling.
6. **VIRGO** (Ruled by Mercury): Work & service, health, employees, psychic sensitivity, spiritual growth.
7. **LIBRA** (Ruled by Venus): Partnership, awareness of others, the 'mirror", the worthy opponent.
8. **SCORPIO** (Ruled by Mars & Pluto): Resources of others, business activity, debts, taxes & insurance, death.
9. **SAGITTARIUS** (Ruled by Jupiter): Higher education, foreign travel, expansion, religion, in-laws. legal matters.
10. **CAPRICORN** (Ruled by Saturn): Profession, reputation, public image, leadership, control, "being on top of it".
11. **AQUARIUS** (Ruled by Uranus) : Friends, hopes & wishes, shared creativity, cooperative efforts, clubs & groups.
12. **PISCES** (Ruled by Neptune): Completion of unfinished business, bringing order out of chaos, self-perception, the house of self-undoing, self-imprisonment.

"WHERE" the ENERGIES operate!

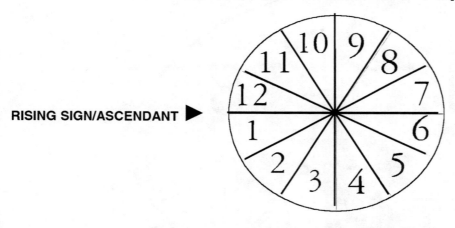

RISING SIGN/ASCENDANT ▶

The 12 NATURAL HOUSES of the Zodiac

Each house is given a number from one to twelve, the first house cusp is located at what would be nine o'clock on a clock-face, then, moving counter-clockwise, numbering off around the chart.

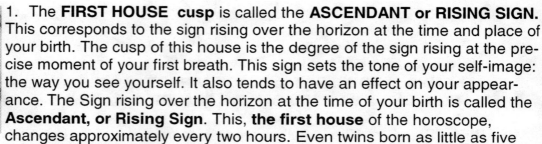

1. The **FIRST HOUSE** cusp is called the **ASCENDANT or RISING SIGN.** This corresponds to the sign rising over the horizon at the time and place of your birth. The cusp of this house is the degree of the sign rising at the precise moment of your first breath. This sign sets the tone of your self-image: the way you see yourself. It also tends to have an effect on your appearance. The Sign rising over the horizon at the time of your birth is called the **Ascendant, or Rising Sign**. This, **the first house** of the horoscope, changes approximately every two hours. Even twins born as little as five minutes apart could have different ascendants, which would make a real difference in their horoscopes and so in their personalities.

The **Rising Sign** governs your outer personality and physical attributes. It describes and represents your physical body, self-image and, to a considerable extent, how others see you. It also affects your health issues and the type of illnesses you may experience. The Rising Sign rules the First house, so its ruling planet is usually designated the ruler of the horoscope. Unless poorly aspected or otherwise weak in comparison with other important planets, such as the planet ruling your Sun Sign (the Sun-ruler), this ruling planet is the most important one in your chart.

2. The **SECOND HOUSE** is called the house of values. It represents and describes your material assets, how you handle monetary income, and the potential ways it may be earned. It also indicates what helps you to have self-esteem and describes financial priorities you establish throughout life.

3. The **THIRD HOUSE** describes your mental state, intellectual orientation, self-expression and communication, early education, mechanical dexterity and skills, immediate environment (neighborhood), and siblings. It describes the lower mind and how it works, your daily activities & physical actions, and transportation, especially within your immediate environment. The third house may also describe the job or health of your mother.

4. The **FOURTH HOUSE** describes your residence, domestic environment, and family members, especially your father (although it can also strongly indicate the nature of your mother). It indicates the beginning as well as the end of various cycles in your life.

5. The **FIFTH HOUSE** describes your creative talent and imaginative powers, capacity for enjoyment and the pursuit of pleasure, romance, children, and speculative ventures, idealistic or spiritualist tendencies. Many planets in this house can indicate the number of children you might have (of the mind, as well as the body) and that you have a flair for drama.

6. The **SIXTH HOUSE** describes your job, daily responsibilities (paid and unpaid), and those who work for or with you. It also represents your health, and physical fitness. Small animals and the military are two more subjects governed by this house.

7. The **SEVENTH HOUSE** relates to marriage and partnership or joint ventures of any kind. It describes how you interact with people and how others tend to regard you. The seventh house is associated with legal matters, negotiations, contracts, open enemies and all open confrontations, pleasant as well as adversarial.

8. The **EIGHTH HOUSE** is related to taxes, debt, death, legacies, other people's money (credit; investments; insurances and so on) and the income you receive through your marriage or business partner (s). It describes your resourcefulness, and your ability to develop and use material assets as well as personal skills and abilities particularly in joint ventures or partnership projects. The eighth house also indicates sexual attitudes and behavior, your responses to life's mysteries and all matters to do with the end of life.

9. The **NINTH HOUSE** describes higher education, advanced training, publishing, publicity, advertising, politics, foreign travel, foreign studies, religious and philosophical views and activities, and cultural pursuits. It relates to court decisions, a second marriage, and in-laws. To a certain extent the ninth house also describes the job or health of your father.

10. The **TENTH HOUSE ,** or Mid-Heaven (MC), describes your career and other long-range goals, public reputation, superiors and those in authority. It also relates to your mother and her influence in your life. The MC stands for *Medium Coeli*, which is Latin for mid-heaven. The mid-heaven degree is that where the sun reaches its highest point during the day. This degree is usually counted as the cusp of the tenth house.

11. The **ELEVENTH HOUSE** rules friendships, organizations to which you belong, and income derived from self-employment or career (as opposed to wages earned from a job). It relates to the role you play in the lives of others as child, parent, lover, spouse, friend, social or business associate. The eleventh house also describes your hopes and aspirations and capacity for happiness.

12. The **TWELFTH HOUSE** describes the private and hidden side of life; your subconscious mind, dreams, the past, and those who wish you harm or work against your interests. The twelfth house relates to sorrow, disappointment, loss, institutions, secret enemies, solitude or confinement, hidden fears and worry. It also has connection with the job or health of your marriage or business partner.

My NOTES:

_____
_____
_____
_____
_____
_____
_____
_____
_____
_____
_____
_____
_____
_____
_____
_____
_____.

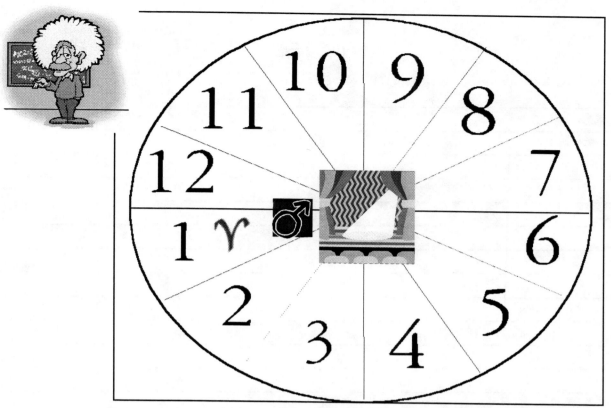

The "NATURAL CHART" The **STAGE WHERE** the **ENERGIES** are operating.

FILL-IN the 12 HOUSES with the SIGNS of the ZODIAC & the PLANETS that Rule those HOUSES:

1. **ARIES** (Ruled by Mars): Self-awareness, personality, physical body, the head, personal power.
2. **TAURUS** (Ruled by Venus) : Self-worth, income, possessions, emotional needs, personal re sources & talents.
3. **GEMINI** (Ruled by Mercury) : Mental activity, short trips, communication, classes, brothers & sisters & neighbors.
4. **CANCER** (Ruled by the Moon): Home & family interests, property, security, roots, end of life, base of operation, the Mother.
5. **LEO** ~(Ruled by the Sun): Creativity, children, new projects, love affairs, fun & pleasure, speculation, gambling.
6. **VIRGO** (Ruled by Mercury): Work & service, health, employees, psychic sensitivity, spiritual growth.
7. **LIBRA** (Ruled by Venus) : Partnership, awareness of others, the 'mirror", the worthy opponent.
8. **SCORPIO** (Co-Ruled by Mars & Pluto): Resources of others, business activity, debts, taxes & insurance, death.
9. **SAGITTARIUS** (Ruled by Jupiter): Higher education, foreign travel, expansion, religion, in-laws. legal matters.
10. **CAPRICORN** (Ruled by Saturn): Profession, reputation, public image, leadership, control, "being on top of it".
11. **AQUARIUS** (Ruled by Uranus): Friends, hopes & wishes, shared creativity, cooperative efforts, clubs & groups.
12. **PISCES** (Ruled by Neptune): Completion of unfinished business, bringing order out of chaos, self-perception, the house of self-undoing, self-imprisonment.

My NOTES

A REVIEW

The SIGNS and Their SYMBOLS

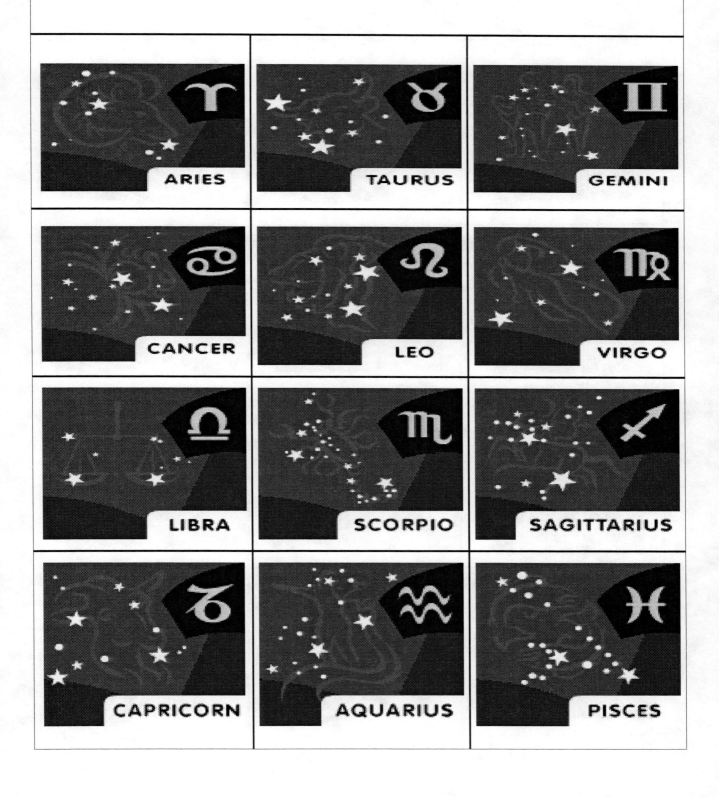

SYMBOLS for the PLANETS

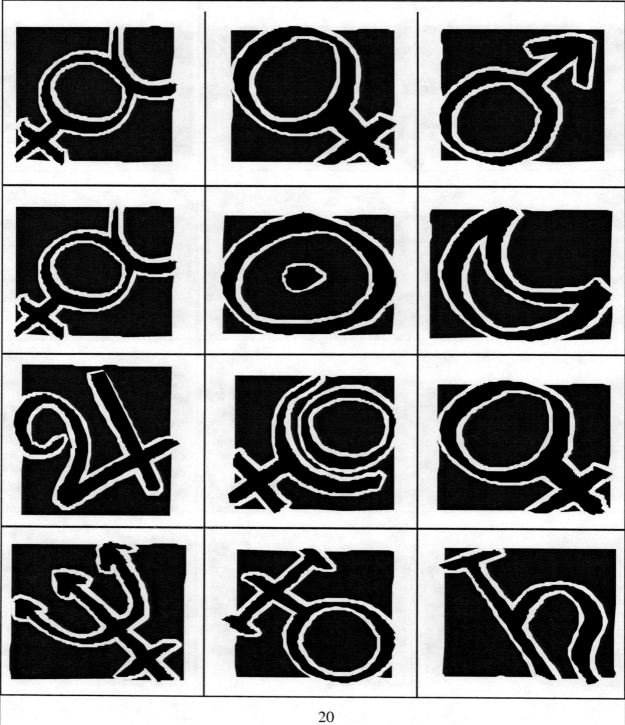

Fill-IN the Planetary RULERS for
The SIGNS & SYMBOLS

 Ruled by the Planet

_____

ARIES

 Ruled by the Planet

_____

TAURUS

 Ruled by the Planet

_____

GEMINI

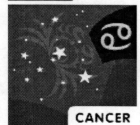 Ruled by the

_____

CANCER

 Ruled by the

_____

LEO

 Ruled by the Planet

_____

VIRGO

 Ruled by the Planet

_____

LIBRA

 Ruled by the Planet

_____

SCORPIO

 Ruled by the Planet

_____

SAGITTARIUS

 Ruled by the Planet

_____

CAPRICORN

 Ruled by the Planet

_____

AQUARIUS

 Ruled by the Planet

_____

PISCES

Name The Planets
by Their Symbols

_____   _____   _____

_____   _____   _____

_____   _____   _____

_____   _____   _____

Match the names of the
signs to the symbol
for the sign

Aries
Taurus
Gemini
Cancer
Leo
Virgo
Libra
Scorpio
Sagittarius
Capricorn
Aquarius
Pisces

The Planets & Their Meanings

 The SUN is masculine in its nature and represents our vitality, sense of individuality, creative energy, inner-self and essential values. The sun urges us to be and to create. The ego is strong here and there is a need to be recognized.

The SUN was in the sign of _____ when I was born.

The MOON is feminine in its nature and represents our automatic or conditioned emotional responses, subconscious predispositions, and self-image The moon urges us to feel inner support, domestic and emotional security. The need for emotional tranquility and sense of belonging, to feel right about self.

The MOON was in the sign of _____ when I was born.

MERCURY has no sexuality. It represents communication, the logical or rational mind, and our reasoning ability. Mercury urges us to express our perceptions and intelligence through skill or speech. The need to establish connections with others and the need to learn.

MERCURY was in the sign of _____ when I was born.

VENUS is feminine in its nature and represents physical likes and dislikes, the exchange of energy, sharing. Venus attracts and urges us to interact socially, to express affection and to seek pleasure. The need to feel close to another, to feel comfort and harmony, to give affection.

VENUS was in the sign of _____ when I was born.

MARS is masculine in its nature and represents physical desire, our will toward action, initiative, physical energy, and drive. Mars urges us to be self-assertive and aggressive, it is our sexual urge, to act decisively. It symbolizes the need to achieve one's desires, the need for physical and sexual excitement, anger.

MARS was in the sign of _____ when I was born.

JUPITER represents expansion, grace, mental growth, good fortune. Jupiter urges us toward a larger order or to connect with something greater than self. It symbolizes the need for faith, trust and confidence in life and self, the need to improve oneself.

JUPITER was in the sign of _____ when I was born.

SATURN, the planet of limitations, represents the principles of contractions, effort and control. Saturn urges us to defend our own structure and integrity, it is the urge toward safety and security through tangible achievement. It symbolizes the need for social approval and to rely on one's own resources and efforts.

SATURN was in the sign of _____ when I was born.

URANUS represents individualistic freedom and urges one toward originality, differentiation and independence from tradition. It symbolizes the need for change, variety, excitement and expression without restraint. Often called the rebel, it is the planet of extremes and is futuristic. Wherever Uranus is in your chart...expect the unexpected!

URANUS was in the sign of _____ when I was born.

NEPTUNE is often referred to as the planet of "fog & illusion". It represents transcendent freedom and urges us to escape the limitations of the material world. It symbolizes the need to experience a oneness with life, and to merge with the whole. Neptune's energies seem to heal and to absolve...to wash away.

NEPTUNE was in the sign of _____ when I was born.

PLUTO, the planet most associated with power, represents the power to transform, transmute and eliminate. It urges us to penetrate the core of experience and to change things. It symbolizes the need to refine oneself and to release the old and rebuild the new.

PLUTO was in the sign of _____ when I was born.

Your RISING SIGN is determined by the HOUR of your BIRTH. It is the starting point of your chart and is located at the 9 PM position of the regular clock. It represents how you project yourself and therefore, how others might perceive you at first glance. It also seems to represent how you view the world. My RISING SIGN is_____.

The NODES: These are points in the heavens where the path of the sun and the moon cross, having an 18 year approximate cycle. In our charts, they seem to represent beginnings & endings. ☊ The NORTH NODE: This point in our chart represents what we are trying to accomplish and work towards in our journey of life. My

NORTH NODE IS:_____. ☋ The SOUTH NODE seems to represent past-life accomplishments, what comes easy to us and what we are trying to leave behind. My SOUTH NODE is_____.

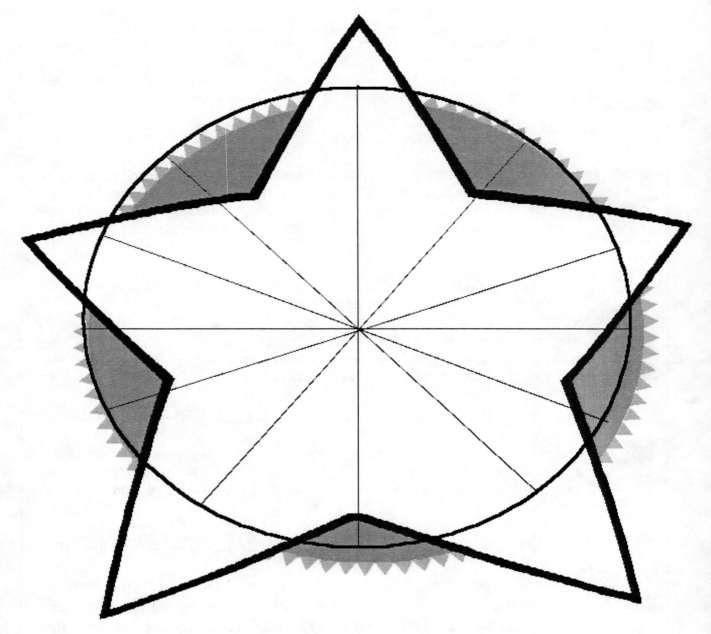

Let's Practice!

Look at YOUR printed Astrology chart
and copy into this wheel:

1. The planets
2. The signs they are in, as well as
3. The correct houses they are in.

CONGRATULATIONS!

Chapter 2

1. The 4 ELEMENTS & Their Key Concepts
2. The QUADRUPLICITIES & their Qualities:
   Air, Fire, Earth & Water
   Let's See what you Remember!
3. The TRIPLICITIES & Their Qualities:
   Cardinal Fixed & Mutable
   Let's See what you Remember!
4. Flash Cards for Reviewing

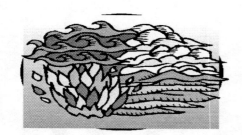

The 4 ELEMENTS & their KEY CONCEPTS

Astrological signs are categorized by their elemental identities of **AIR, FIRE EARTH** and **WATER** and these basic elements refer to the four basic personality types. These four **ELEMENTS** are also known as the **QUADRUPLICITIES**. They are considered the building blocks of existence at all levels. They represent a much broader range of experience than the "chemical elements" of modern science, and should not be confused with them. These **QUALITIES** are also known as the **TRIPLICITIES** and are usually interpreted in conjunction with the **ELEMENTS** or **QUADRIPLICITIES**. By knowing only this information in a person's chart, one could tell quite a bit about the personality drives and needs of that individual!

TRIPLICITIES▶ ELEMENT ▼	CARDINAL Initiating, Creative	FIXED Stubborn, Strong-willed Determined	MUTABLE Flexible, changeable
AIR Intellect & Communication detached	LIBRA	AQUARIUS	GEMINI
FIRE Spirit & Energy Inspiring	ARIES	LEO	SAGITTARIUS
EARTH Material Security Practical Organized	CAPRICORN	TAURUS	VIRGO
WATER Nurturing Emotional security & psychic	CANCER	SCORPIO	PISCES

The 4 ELEMENTS as PERSONALITY TYPES

AIR   **FIRE**   **EARTH**   **WATER**

In Astrology, the elements refer to the four basic personality types:

Our personality is made up of many different qualities and components. Looking at what the major ELEMENTS in your chart, is a simple way of explaining your basic drives in life.

The AIR signs (GEMINI, LIBRA & AQUARIUS) generally are mental and enjoy communicating. They will cool you or blow you away! AIR sign people tend to be detached. They need INTELLECTUAL FREEDOM.

The FIRE signs (ARIES, LEO & SAGITTARIUS) like to inspire and generally are physical and like activity. They need to have their PHYSICAL FREEDOM. They are very much like the element FIRE, which changes shape and can warm you or burn you!

AIR & FIRE elements are considered to be very compatible (AIR fans FIRE). They both need FREEDOM. People with a lot of AIR & FIRE in their chart are very much like those elements. AIR & FIRE cannot be contained...or it dies!

The EARTH signs (TAURUS, VIRGO & CAPRICORN) are "down to earth, practical, usually very organized and like material comforts. They are looking for MATERIAL SECURITY in life. They like order and respond well to having boundaries.

The WATER signs (CANCER, SCORPIO & PISCES) are very sensitive, psychic & emotional. They are looking for EMOTIONAL SECURITY. They also respond well to boundaries, in order to feel secure.

The right amount of WATER & EARTH will create a beautiful garden, too much will create a mud puddle and not enough water, will become a desert. The elements EARTH & WATER need a container...or they tend to get dissolve or get scattered.

The 4 ELEMENTS & Their QUALITIES

AIR FIRE EARTH WATER

The **AIR** signs represent the world of ideas, ideals and communication.

Those of you who have a lot of AIR in your charts, are lovers of TRUTH. You tend to be logical, rational liberal, intellectual, cool, objective, detached and abstract. You make stimulating conversationalists and are natural philosophers. You have a strong capacity and need, to understand everything. To you, the idea is everything...feelings must be subjugated to the idea. You see what would be...from an idealistic viewpoint. You will also make tremendous sacrifices for the ideal. Your cool wit, clarity and transparency are noticeable. You are usually optimistic, objective and reasonable. On the other hand, you can be emotionally childlike, naïve, not very flexible, an incurable romantic and intense. Air signs, for the most part, tend to be socially pleasant, needing companionship, versatile and they enjoy the exchange of ideas. If there are too many air planets in the chart, you can be superficial and lacking in stability and continuity. You can be impractical and inconsistent in your attitudes and you may even be unreliable. You may take chances in life, and your minds tend to concerns of peace. You may have to depend on others for the more practical concerns in life. You tend to be regarded as unifiers and peacemakers, because of your ability to remain cool, detached and analytical. It is your function to bring together and balance personalities who would otherwise not be able to coexist. You will either cool others off ... or blow them away!

The AIR TRIPLITITY: GEMINI LIBRA AQUARIUS

GEMINI is concerned with day to day matters, brothers and sisters. Gemini seeks to effect unity by revealing the unity of cause, assuming also that all things have similar beginning and consequently similar destiny.

LIBRA is concerned with partnerships, marriage, fairness and balance. Libra seeks to effect unity by uniting lives and causing them to blend their individuality through actual partnership or marriage.

AQUARIUS is concerned with friendships and humanitarian causes. Aquarius seeks to effect unity by revealing common motives, thus establishing the bond of mutual interests and mutual responsibilities.

The 4 ELEMENTS & Their QUALITIES

AIR   FIRE   EARTH   WATER

The **FIRE** element represents the creative, inspirational nature of man.

The FIRE signs have inexhaustible amounts of physical energy and tend to be impulsive, dynamic, sharp, magnetic and sometimes oppressively forceful. People dominated by this element can be impulsive, sharp, dissecting and iconoclastic. Your minds are brilliant, original and suitable to instruct others in science and philosophy. Fire is hot and volatile and cannot be contained in shape, size or form. Fire changes shape and form very rapidly and it burns everything it touches. Its purpose is to disintegrate and continually burn away the dead energy and liberate spirit from form. Those of you who have a lot of fire in your chart, have the ability to shape creative things out of random possibilities. You have *vision*, you are usually *dramatic* and your *enthusiasm* is contagious. You tend to be *inspirational, self-motivated* and *future oriented*. Your dreams are sacred to you. You can be unpredictable, romantic and ardent. Your intuition helps to bring light into darkness. You have a need to conquer the world in grand style...to you, all of the world is your stage! You are a restless traveler who senses that maturity is seeing, knowing and understanding, You will warm others or burn them!

 The FIRE TRIPLICITY: ARIES LEO SAGITTARIUS

ARIES is concerned with the building of the body of man. In Aries, the fire is red and angry, there is great heat and the smoldering flames may, at any time, break forth into a terrible combustion.

LEO is concerned with procreation of the mind as well as the body. In Leo, the flame is golden and luminous and burns steadily so that all may benefit from its warm and illuminating glow.

SAGITTARIUS is concerned with the development of the higher mind. In Sagittarius, the fire flashes with inspiration and its clear blue flame lights the innermost recesses of the mind, many times with prophetic accuracy!

The 4 ELEMENTS & Their QUALITIES

AIR   FIRE   EARTH   WATER

The **EARTH** elements represent the physical, material worlds
of reality and one's environment.

Those of you who are made up of mostly earth energies, tend to be practical, conservative, realistic, disci-
plined, dutiful, responsible and committed. You tend to
be interested in only what works, you are factual and
live in the present. You will only reach for what is possible. You are quite fond of security, money and
status. Maturity to you is synonymous with taking responsibility in the tangible world. Productivity, effi-
ciency, reliability, diligence, patience and organization
are your keywords. On the other hand, because you
fear disorder and chaos, you can tend to be dogmatic, narrow-minded and
overly obsessive. You are the eternal old man or old woman. Through your
over-insistence of the practical, you can crush creativity. You have remarkable recuperative powers, in fact, most of you are somewhat concerned with
health, for the body is the immediate environment of the life evolving within.
You tend to promote the conservation and concentration of resources. Since
you tend to be more passive than active, you can be inhibited in your self-
expression. Being the heaviest of the four elements, you tend to be practical,
conservative and are great lovers of material goods. You will either help others to grow beautiful crops...or you will bury them!

 The EARTH TRIPLICITY: TAURUS VIRGO CAPRICORN

TAURUS is concerned with our most basic security needs: home, food, sex
and physical comfort. Taurus symbolizes the broad and fertile plains, hills and
valleys as well as the deserts, ready to be plowed by the great ox, warm with
sunshine and bright with flowers.

VIRGO is most concerned with health and service-oriented occupational matters. Virgo best symbolizes the deep valleys where nameless secrets are
hidden, and a feeling of depth prevails.

CAPRICORN is concerned with the material world, success and their social
standing in the community in which they reside. Capricorn symbolizes the
rugged mountains that over-shadow all...bringing a sense of timelessness,
stability and majesty.

The 4 ELEMENTS & Their QUALITIES

AIR   FIRE   EARTH   WATER

The **WATER** signs represent the completion of things, the end of life and its mysteries, the emotional concerns of life, and the psychic nature of man.

Those of you who are made up mostly of WATER energies, are very emotionally perceptive and attuned to subtle "vibrations or energies". You tend to instinctive, fluid, imaginative, creative and profound. Feelings are everything... the idea must be bent to the feeling. You see the here and the now. Because you cannot bear isolation or rejection, you can be possessive. Your acute sensitivity and heartfelt intelligence helps you to know what people need and how the feel. You will make sacrifices for loved ones. On the other hand, you can be emotional blackmailers. You are capable of bending the truth with veiled insults and disguised criticisms. You can be manipulative, and some of you have a tendency to create guilt in loved ones for not giving as much as you do.

Water signs are changeable, impressionistic, sensitive and emotional. Water is one of the most powerful of the four elements...what it cannot go through, it will go around or over! Because of water's fluidic nature, water signs tend to be easily influenced and susceptible to moods and impressions. You will either refresh others or drown them!

The WATER TRIPLICITY: CANCER SCORPIO PISCES

Water exists in three states...fluid, solid or steam

CANCER represents the fluid state, the personality is changeable and fluctuating and subject to countless phases.

SCORPIO represents water in its frozen state, solid and least responsive. Scorpios tend to be deep and mysterious.

PISCES represents water in its most vaporous state, the physical rising towards the metaphysical.

Let's see what you remember!

The AIR signs are: _____, _____, _____.
The AIR signs in my chart are: (EXAMPLE: Mercury in Gemini)

_____
_____
_____.

The FIRE signs are _____, _____, _____
The FIRE signs in my chart are: (Example Sun in Aries)

_____
_____
_____

The EARTH signs are: _____, _____, _____
The EARTH signs in my chart are: (Example: Saturn in Taurus)

_____
_____
_____

The WATER signs are _____, _____, _____
The WATER signs in my chart are: (Example: Moon in Cancer)

_____
_____
_____.

PLANETS I have in each ELEMENT

I have _____ PLANETS in AIR
I have _____ PLANETS in FIRE
I have _____ PLANETS in EARTH
I have _____ PLANETS in WATER

The Triplicities:
(Cardinal ■ Fixed ■ Mutable & Their Key Concepts)

The CARDINAL Signs: Aries Cancer Libra Capricorn

Keywords: As a group, these signs are ambitious, ardent, energetic, initiatory, progressive, pioneering, organizing, independent, proud, they dislike menial positions. Their minds are quick, fertile and insatiable. In the more undeveloped types, they are likely to hasty, inconsiderate, reckless, destructive and domineering.

ARIES ♈ : Gives the desire to achieve through force, to overcome obstacles with dramatic gestures, aggressive cooperation and great devotion to person and causes; they love to dispute! My Chart shows that I have these planets in the sign of ARIES:_____, _____, _____, _____, _____, _____, _____, _____,

CANCER ♋: This sign has silent and inconspicuous ambitions; these people are often the power behind achievements of others; although they have a strong emotional nature, there is often remarkable business ability.
My Chart shows that I have these planets in the sign of CANCER :_____, _____, _____, _____, _____, _____.

LIBRA ♎: These people give solidarity and cooperation in ambitions. They are inclined to partnerships and various combinations in which several work together for a mutual end. My chart show that I have these planets in the sign of LIBRA: _____, _____, _____, _____, _____,

CAPRICORN ♑: These people have political, scientific and scholarly ambition; they may become a public servant. There is continual effort and there can be a tremendous will power often with arrogance. My chart show that I have these planets in the sign of CAPRICORN_____,_____,_____, _____,

The **CARDINAL Signs** are most powerful when on the angles (1st, 4th, 7th 10 house cusps) of the houses where their qualities will dominate the life of the native. They are also powerful when there is a majority of planets in the cardinal signs. If the sun is in a cardinal sign, it will impel the life toward fulfillment of ambitions.

I have (#) _____ PLANETS in CARDINAL SIGNS. My chart shows that I have MY CARDINAL planets in these houses : _____, _____, _____, _____, _____, _____.

Let's see what you remember!

The **CARDINAL SIGNS:** _____, _____, _____, _____

KEYWORDS: As a group, these signs are:

_____

_____.

The "shadow" side and in the more undeveloped types, CARDINAL signs are likely to be :_____

_____

_____.

My chart shows that I have the PLANETS _____, _____, _____, _____, _____, _____, _____ in the sign of ARIES.

My chart shows that I have the PLANETS _____, _____, _____, _____, _____ , _____, _____ in the sign of CANCER

My chart shows that I have the PLANETS _____, _____, _____, _____, _____ , _____, _____ in the sign of LIBRA:

My chart shows that I have the PLANETS _____, _____, _____, _____, _____ , _____, _____ in the sign of CAPRICORN

I have (#) _____ PLANETS in CARDINAL SIGNS

My CARDINAL PLANETS are in the (house #) _____, _____, _____, _____, _____, _____, _____ HOUSES.

The Triplicities:
(Cardinal ■ Fixed ■ Mutable & Their Key Concepts)

The FIXED SIGNS: Taurus Leo Scorpio Aquarius

Keywords: As a group, these signs can be dogmatic, unyielding, determined, organized, accumulative, ulterior, firm, conservative, laborious, dignified, proud, thrifty, self-absorbed, executive, habit-bound, bossy and temperamental. Their minds are penetrating, analytical, secretive; they tend to achieve results slowly, but surely, with excellent memories. In the more undeveloped types, they can be stubborn, bigoted, sluggish, egotistical, tyrannical and too concerned with details.

TAURUS ♉**:** This sign desires to retain their own opinions, they are inclined to jealousy, can be prideful and in some types, prudish; they wear down the opposition by sheer tenacity and will never admit defeat. My Chart shows that I have these planets in the sign of TAURUS:_____, _____, _____, _____, _____, _____.

LEO ♌ **:** these people tend to stick to the ideal, they are willing to suffer for principle, they are determined in the face of obstacles, but they can become austere and somewhat distant. My Chart shows that I have these planets in the sign of LEO:_____, _____, _____, _____, _____, _____,

SCORPIO ♏**:** This sign tends to conclusions of a scientific or psychological nature; they regard no authority other than experience, and their fixity is likely to interfere with the rights of others. My Chart shows that I have these planets in the sign of SCORPIO:_____, _____, _____, _____, _____, _____,

AQUARIUS ♒**:** This sign tends to live life on whims; they cannot be moved from the notion which serves them at the moment. They can change their minds with alarming rapidity, generally accomplishing this feat without experiencing any loss of popularity. My Chart shows that I have these planets in the sign of AQUARIUS:_____, _____, _____, _____, _____,

The **FIXED Signs** are most powerful when on the angles, where their qualities assume some of the dignities of the cardinal signs and dominate the life of the native. They are also powerful when a majority of planets are in fixed signs. If the sun is in a fixed sign, it will impel the life to expend its entire span in the service of some definite opinion.

I have (#) _____ PLANETS in FIXED SIGNS. My **FIXED Planets** are in these houses: _____, _____, _____, _____, _____, _____.

Let's see what you remember!

The **FIXED** signs: _____, _____, _____, _____

KEYWORDS: As a group, these signs are:

_____
_____.

The "shadow" side and in the more undeveloped types, MUTABLE signs are likely to be :_____
_____
_____.

My chart shows that I have the PLANETS _____, _____,
_____, _____, _____, _____,
_____ in the sign of TAURUS.

My chart shows that I have the PLANETS _____, _____,
_____, _____, _____, _____,
_____ in the sign of LEO.

My chart shows that I have the PLANETS _____, _____,
_____, _____, _____, _____,
_____ in the sign of SCORPIO.

My chart shows that I have the PLANETS _____, _____,
_____, _____, _____, _____,
_____ in the sign of AQUARIUS.

I have (#) _____ PLANETS in FIXED SIGNS

My **FIXED PLANETS** are in the (house #) _____, _____,
_____, _____, _____,
_____, _____, _____HOUSES

The Triplicities:

(Cardinal ■ Fixed ■ Mutable & Their Key Concepts)

The MUTABLE Signs: Gemini Virgo Sagittarius Pisces

Keywords: As a group they can be changeable, subtle, inconstant, susceptible, regretful, sympathetic, retiring, rhythmic, tedious, intuitive, diplomatic, critical, judicial, humanitarian, methodical, comprehending, impractical. Their minds are flexible, ingenious, irresolute and they often work as commentators, counselor and advisors. In an undeveloped type, or when in their shadow side, they may be crafty, deceptive and have ulterior motives.

GEMINI Ⅱ: These people can be superficial and are inclined to unnecessary repetitions, they may do too much day-dreaming and worrying for their own good, they can also be absent-minded. They are quite capable of doing two or more things at once. My Chart shows that I have these planets in the sign of GEMINI:_____,
_____, _____, _____, _____,

VIRGO ♍ : These people tend to be analytical and critical; they can be either very secretive or else attach themselves to a stronger willed person and become dependent; they can be easily influenced. My Chart shows that I have these planets in the sign of VIRGO:_____, _____, _____,
_____, _____, _____, _____,

SAGITTARIUS ♐ : These people are open and obvious; they are fond of the beautiful, harmonious and the peaceful; there can be some pride, a tendency to pomp and dignity and can also exhibit an attachment to custom and family. My Chart shows that I have these planets in the sign of SAGITTARIUS:_____,
_____, _____, _____, _____,

PISCES ♓ : These people have powerful imaginations, which are apt to control their lives, they can be talkative and quite possibly lazy; typically, they become servants to the spiritual, legal and medical needs of mankind. My Chart shows that I have these planets in the sign of PISCES:_____, _____, _____,
_____, _____, _____, _____,

The **MUTABLE** signs are most powerful when on the angles, where their qualities assume some of the active elements of the cardinal signs and dominate the life of the native. They are also powerful when a majority of planets are posited in them. If the sun is in a mutable sign, it will impel the life toward interaction and distribution.

I have (#) _____ PLANETS in MUTABLE SIGNS. My Chart shows that my MUTABLE planets are in these houses:_____, _____,
_____, _____, _____, _____.

Let's see what you remember!

The **MUTABLE** signs: _____, _____, _____, _____

KEYWORDS: As a group, these signs are:

_____
_____.

The "shadow" side and in the more undeveloped types, MUTABLE signs are likely to be :_____
_____
_____.

My chart shows that I have the PLANETS _____, _____,
_____, _____, _____, _____ ,
_____ in the sign of GEMINI.

My chart shows that I have the PLANETS _____, _____,
_____, _____, _____ , _____,
_____ in the sign of VIRGO

My chart shows that I have the PLANETS _____, _____,
_____, _____, _____ , _____,
_____ in the sign of SAGITTARIUS

My chart shows that I have the PLANETS _____, _____,
_____, _____, _____ , _____,
_____ in the sign of PISCES.

I have (#) _____ PLANETS in MUTABLE SIGNS

My MUTABLE PLANETS are in the (house #) _____, _____,
_____, _____, _____,
_____, _____ , _____HOUSES

A Key to The 4 ELEMENTS & Their QUALITIES

 **AIR:** Keywords are detached, cool, analytical, mental.

Cardinal Air: LIBRA: Harmonization of all polarities for self-completion. A planet in this sign will be colored by balance, impartiality and tact.

Fixed Air: AQUARIUS: Detached coordination of all people and concepts. A planet in this sign will be colored by individualism, freedom and extremism.

Mutable Air: GEMINI: Immediate perception, verbalization of all connection. A planet in this sign will be colored by changeableness, curiosity, talkativeness and friendliness.

 **FIRE:** Keywords are warmth, enthusiasm, inspirational.

Cardinal Fire: ARIES: Single-pointed release of energy toward new experiences. A planet in this sign will have a self-willed urge for action and self-assertion.

Fixed Fire: LEO: Sustained warmth , loyalty and radiant vitalization. A planet in this sign will be colored by pride and strong urge for recognition, sense of drama.

Mutable Fire: Sagittarius: Restless aspiration propelling one toward an ideal. A planet in this sign will be colored by their beliefs, generalizations and ideals.

 **EARTH:** Keywords are organized, practical, down-to-earth.

Cardinal Earth: Capricorn: Determination to get things done. A planet in this sign will be colored by self-control, caution, reserve and ambition.

Fixed Earth: Taurus: Depth of appreciation, attuned to immediate physical sensations. A planet in this sign will be colored by possessiveness, retentiveness and stability.

Mutable Earth: Virgo : Spontaneous helpfulness, humility and the need to serve. A planet in this sign will be colored by perfectionism, analysis and fine discrimination.

 WATER: Keywords are emotional, sensitive, psychic.

Cardinal Water: Cancer: Instinctive nurturing and protective empathy. A planet in this sign will be colored by feeling, reserve, moods, sensitivity and self-protection.

Fixed Water: Scorpio: Penetration through intense emotional power. A planet in this sign will be colored by compulsive desires, depth, controlled passion and secrecy.

Mutable Water: Pisces: Healing compassion for all that suffer. A planet in this sign will be colored by soul yearnings, oneness, inspiration and vulnerability.

My NOTES:

_____
_____
_____
_____
_____
_____
_____
_____
_____
_____
_____
_____
_____
_____
_____
_____
_____
_____
_____
_____
_____
_____

MAKE FLASH CARDS

ARIES

TAURUS

GEMINI

CANCER

LEO

VIRGO

LIBRA

SCORPIO

MAKE FLASH CARDS

♉ ♈

♋ ♊

♍ ♌

♏ ♎

MAKE FLASH CARDS

SAGITTARIUS

CAPRICORN

AQUARIUS

PISCES

CARDINAL

FIXED

MUTABLE

THE ELEMENTS

MAKE FLASH CARDS

♑

♓

TAURUS	ARIES
LEO	CANCER
SCORPIO	LIBRA
AQUARIUS	CAPRICORN

AIR	GEMINI
FIRE	VIRGO
EARTH	SAGITTARIUS
WATER	PISCES

CHAPTER   3

1. More about the HOUSES of the NATURAL CHART
2. Coloring the Natural Chart by ELEMENTS
3. ASTRO KEYS
4. The Ascendant or RISING SIGN
5. The Moon's NODES

More about The HOUSES of the NATURAL CHART

The HOUSES in the NATURAL chart represent the STAGE upon which we act out our PLANETARY ENERGIES.

In Chapter 1 we touched lightly upon what each house represents. Basically, they represent the different aspects of what one needs in order to experience a full life. In this chapter we are going to look at those houses in a different light.

We must first start with what is called the "natural chart". By using color, it is much easier to "see" at a glance, which houses exhibit earthy, airy, emotional or fiery qualities.

AIR signs = BLUE
FIRE signs = RED
WATER signs = GREEN
EARTH signs = BROWN

CARDINAL Houses: 1, 4. 7, 10
FIXED Houses: 2, 5, 8, 11
MUTABLE Houses: 3, 6, 9, 12

The NATURAL CHART
This is the **STAGE** or the **ENVIRONMENT** "**WHERE**" the **ENERGIES** are operating

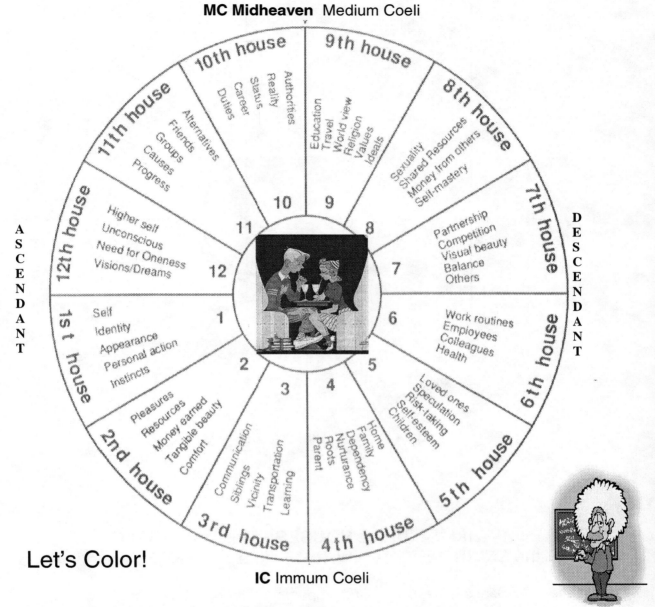

MC Midheaven Medium Coeli

10th house: Authorities, Reality, Status, Career, Duties

9th house: Education, Travel, World view, Religion, Values, Ideals

8th house: Sexuality, Shared Resources, Money from others, Self-mastery

11th house: Alternatives, Friends, Groups, Causes, Progress

7th house: Partnership, Competition, Visual beauty, Balance, Others

12th house: Higher self, Unconscious, Need for Oneness, Visions/Dreams

6th house: Work routines, Employees, Colleagues, Health

ASCENDANT

DESCENDANT

1st house: Self, Identity, Appearance, Personal action, Instincts

5th house: Loved ones, Speculation, Risk-taking, Self-esteem, Children

2nd house: Pleasures, Resources, Money earned, Tangible beauty, Comfort

4th house: Home, Family, Dependency, Nurturance, Roots, Parent

3rd house: Communication, Siblings, Vicinity, Transportation, Learning

IC Immum Coeli

Let's Color!

1st House ARIES: CARDINAL FIRE color me RED
2nd House TAURUS: FIXED EARTH color me BROWN
3rd House GEMINI: MUTABLE AIR color me BLUE
4th House CANCER: CARDINAL WATER color me GREEN
5th House LEO: FIXED FIRE color me RED
6th House VIRGO: MUTABLE EARTH color me BROWN
7th House LIBRA: CARDINAL AIR color me BLUE
8th House SCORPIO: FIXED WATER color me GREEN
9th House SAGITTARIUS: MUTABLE FIRE color me RED
10th House CAPRICORN: CARDINAL EARTH color me BROWN
11th House AQUARIUS: FIXED AIR color me BLUE
12th House PISCES: MUTABLE WATER color me GREEN

Mid Heaven

ASTRO KEYS

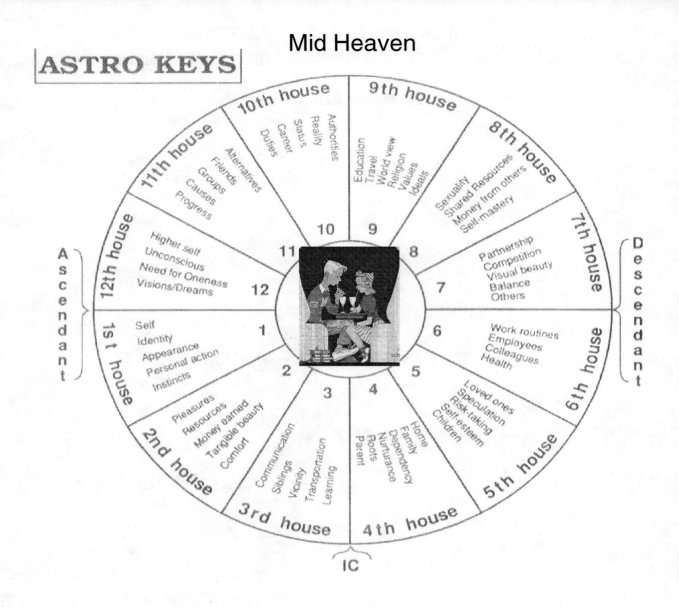

The NATURAL HOUSES: This is the STAGE or the ENVIRONMENT "WHERE" the ENERGIES are operating

1st House ARIES: assertive, brave, first, impetuous, energetic, self-oriented
2nd House TAURUS: comfortable, deliberate, dependable, placid, possessive, sensual
3rd House GEMINI: fluent, versatile, curious, intermittent, clever, nimble, quick, nervous
4th House CANCER: nurturing, warm, dependent, sympathetic, protective, security-oriented
5th House LEO: creative, risk-takers, charismatic, fun-loving, generous, exciting, bossy
6th House VIRGO: service-oriented, efficient, exacting, discreet, critical, organized
7th House LIBRA: fair, cooperative, fence-sitters, competitive, aesthetic, artistic, procrastinators
8th House SCORPIO: penetrating, intense, resourceful, powerful, compulsive, jealous
9th House SAGITTARIUS: benevolent, optimistic, extravagant, enthusiastic, idealistic, visionary
10th House CAPRICORN: responsible, formal, traditional, career-oriented, authoritative
11th House AQUARIUS: unique, rebellious, futuristic, independent, inventive, objective, detached
12th House PISCES: compassionate, mystical, illusory, sensitive, spiritual, dreamy, reclusive

Let's see what you remember!

It is generally considered that one spends more time and attention to the matters of the houses in which you have planets located. If you don't have any planets in a house, it means that your energies are not focused in those areas of your life...until a TRANSIT occurs...or you meet someone who has their PLANETS in the SIGNS of your empty houses, then the affairs of that house are activated.

Let's determine what HOUSES are ACTIVE in YOUR Chart! In each HOUSE: Name the PLANETS and the SIGNS those planets are in.

In the FIRST House of ARIES (Ruled by Mars): Self-awareness, personality, physical body, the head, personal power, MY Chart has these SIGNS & PLANETS:

_____
_____
_____.

In the SECOND House of TAURUS (Ruled by Venus): Self-worth, income, possessions, emotional needs, personal resources & talents, MY Chart has these SIGNS & PLANETS :

_____
_____
_____.

In the THIRD House of GEMINI (Ruled by Mercury): Mental activity, short trips, communication, classes, brothers & sisters & neighbors, MY Chart has these SIGNS & PLANETS:

_____
_____
_____.

In the FOURTH House of CANCER (Ruled by the Moon): Home & family interests, property, security, roots, end of life, base of operation, the Mother, MY Chart has these SIGNS & PLANETS:

_____
_____
_____.

In the FIFTH House of LEO (Ruled by the Sun): Creativity, children, new projects, love affairs, fun & pleasure, speculation, gambling, MY Chart has these SIGNS & PLANETS:

_____
_____
_____
_____.

In the 6th House of VIRGO (Ruled by Mercury): Work & service, health, employees, psychic sensitivity, spiritual growth, MY Chart has these SIGNS & PLANETS:

_____
_____
_____.

In the 7th house of LIBRA ~(Ruled by Venus): Partnership, awareness of others, the 'mirror", the worthy opponent, MY Chart has these SIGNS & PLANETS:

_____
_____
_____.

In the EIGHTH House of SCORPIO (Co-ruled by Mars & Pluto): Resources of others, business activity, debts, taxes & insurance, death, MY Chart has these SIGNS & PLANETS :

_____

_____.

In the NINTH House of SAGITTARIUS (Ruled by Jupiter): Higher education, foreign travel, expansion, religion, in-laws. legal matters, MY Chart has these SIGNS & PLANETS :

_____

_____.

In the TENTH House of CAPRICORN (Ruled by Saturn): Profession, reputation, public image, leadership, control, "being on top of it", .MY Chart has these SIGNS & PLANETS :

_____

_____.

In the ELEVENTH House of AQUARIUS (Ruled by Uranus): Friends, hopes & wishes, shared creativity, cooperative efforts, clubs & groups, MY Chart has these SIGNS & PLANETS :

_____

_____.

In the TWELFTH House of PISCES (Ruled by Neptune): Completion of unfinished business, bringing order out of chaos, self-perception, the house of self-undoing, self-imprisonment, MY Chart has these SIGNS & PLANETS :

_____

_____

_____.

MORE NOTES:

The NATURAL CHART

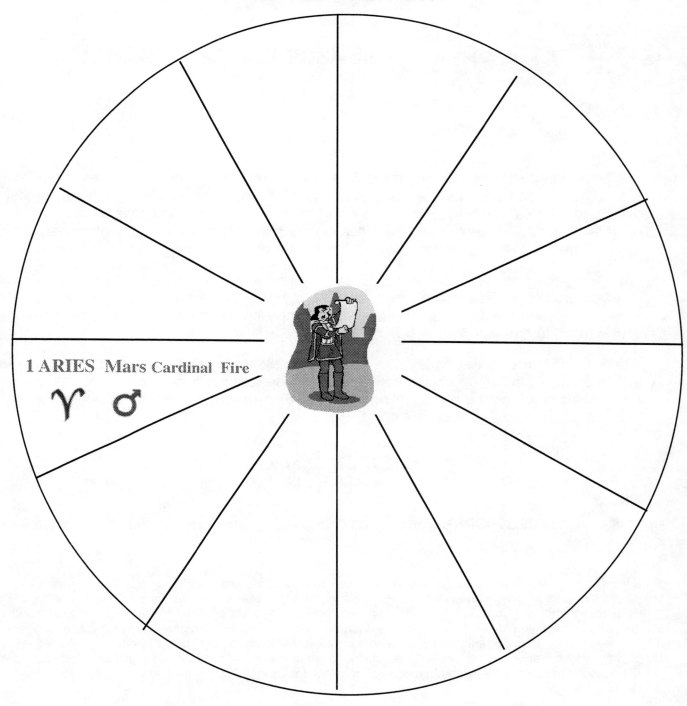

1 ARIES Mars Cardinal Fire

♈ ♂

Let's see what you remember!

Number & Color each HOUSE with the correct ELEMENT color
Include: The SIGN & PLANET which RULES it!

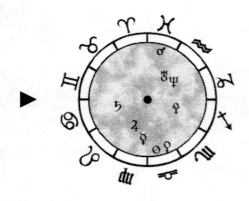

The ASCENDANT or RISING SIGN

The Sign rising over the horizon at the time of your birth is called the Ascendant, or Rising Sign. This sign on the cusp of the first house of the horoscope, changes approximately every two hours. Even twins born as little as five minutes apart could have different ascendants, which would make a real difference in their horoscopes as it regards their personalities and the timing in their lives.

The Rising Sign governs your outer personality and physical attributes. It represents your how you project yourself to the world and, to a considerable extent, how others see you. It also affects your health issues and the type of illnesses you may experience and what the soul is trying to grow towards in this lifetime.

The Rising Sign rules the first house, so its ruling planet is usually designated the ruler of the horoscope. Unless poorly aspected, or otherwise weak in comparison with other important planets, such as the planet ruling your Sun Sign (the Sun-ruler), this ruling planet can be the most important one in your chart.

Rising SIGN Characteristics
(Compliments of Rob Lillett @ astrologycom.com)

ARIES RISING: Tends to be combative or aggressive in their approach to life.

"Me first!"

Aries rising is both positive and dynamic. It endows you with a go-getting, achievement-oriented personality, for you like to be in charge and want to make a big impression under all circumstances. Dedicated to satisfying personal ambitions and pursuing your own ends with complete disregard for the feelings of others doesn't necessarily mean you are always selfish, my dear, but in your haste and eagerness to reach that goal or accomplish that oh so important purpose, it is so easy for you to forget other people's needs, or that what you do may react adversely on others. A powerful inner drive and a strong need for accomplishment, combined with your indomitable Aries courage, urges you to go for things others might think are too risky, too foolish, or just too much work.

Enthusiastic Aries has loads of energy. Once inspired, you rarely hesitate to act and you usually get where you want to go. But be warned! Your lively enthusiasm can get out of hand; you tend to overestimate your own abilities, or the influence you have. In general you maintain an informal approach to life, with easy, open mannerisms and an attitude of "take me as I am". Confronting situations openly and with force need not necessarily brand you as unduly aggressive, for you *can* be quiet and hard-working, sublimating your energy inconspicuously in low-key activities. However your innate restlessness makes it difficult for you to develop an extended concentration span, control your untidiness, or get truly focused and organized.

Ruled by Mars, the fiery warrior, many Arians have reddish hair, ruddy complexions, or a distinctive birthmark on their heads or faces. The Aries mouth has a characteristic down-turn, often associated with a longish face. Being your own boss makes life easier, but you can work in a regular job as long as you don't find the work objectionable and are treated fairly by supervisors. You can be easy-going about many things, but any attempt to ram authority down your throat gets your hackles rising. No doubt the sincerity of your passions makes up to some degree for the rashness of your actions....

You have mechanical abilities or cleverness in one form or another. Fevers, eye strain, accidental injury to the head, skin rashes, overwork, migraine headaches, and insect bites are your most likely physical complaints. Your extremism leads to mental and emotional instability in some situations and you get distinctly stressed out by being thwarted in the pursuit of your goals.

 TAURUS Rising: Tends to present a cautious & conservative approach to life:

Taurus Rising gives you a stubborn streak, combined with a sturdy physique and tremendous physical stamina. Tenacious in getting what you want, your great patience can be the very key to your success. You need, however, to overcome a tendency to procrastinate and a certain difficulty with undesirable habits and behavioral patterns.

Ruled by Venus, planet of sensuality and beauty, you are considered physically attractive. Appreciative as you are, my dears, of good food and fine wines, you may yet avoid an expanding waistline... physical fitness and staying in shape having such a high priority with you. Since you enjoy presenting yourself in the best light, you simply delight in cosmetics and other beauty aids and, no slave to fashion, you select clothes that either show off your best points or are extremely comfortable. Physical comfort is paramount and you do so love the feeling of soft, luxurious materials. Sociable, yet unobtrusive, you enjoy social occasions, especially in the company of friends, even though you can be rather rude and obnoxious when the mood takes you. Some of you may need to overcome a fixation with personal appearance and learn to grow old gracefully. Others may be like little old men or little old women at an early age. On bad days you can be despicably lazy and take little or no interest in your physical appearance or manner of dress.

Taurus has materialistic, status-seeking tendencies. You take pains to hide it, but you can be unduly influenced by the powerful or wealthy. Although your practicality is often self-serving, you are pragmatic and can usually be relied upon for constructive suggestions that help others as much as yourself.

The finer things in life must include art and music, for you are innately talented, with a pleasant, resonant voice. Beware of infections and injuries to your neck and throat and you are subject to earaches and infections.

 GEMINI Rising: Tends to be light-hearted, charming & witty. Can be superficial.

Gemini Rising gives you an adaptable personality and, in general, a wiry, flexible physique. Your airy adaptability to changing circumstances and different people is often so pronounced that your personality and even physical appearance can seem startlingly diverse to different people, and from one time to another. You say what you instinctively know others want to hear. This adaptability can extend to conscious or subconscious imitations of personality traits or the physical appearance of those you admire.

Gemini gives an intellectual orientation, or filter to your life. To others you may often appear interested, but somehow emotionally detached. Physical contacts and mannerisms are quick and restless, and sometimes those rapid movements of yours make it seem as though your mind and body are not connected. You are comfortable doing several things at once, while at the same time appearing not to be paying particular attention to any of them.

Marriage can be difficult for you. For instance, you can be too ready and able to entertain yourself, while your need for more personal freedom can undermine the relationship. In any case you are subject to dual attractions and see no real reason for fidelity, nor indeed do you really expect it from others. Marriage partners, however, may require more passion and personal attention and less independence and intellectual analysis.

Being ruled by Mercury, the mischievous planet of communication, makes you fond of communicating and extremely talkative. Even those with quieter natures are apt to have a great deal of intellectual curiosity. You can absorb a variety of information on all manner of subjects, which you are quite happy to share with anyone willing to listen. You give the impression of mental alertness and understanding, my dear, even though you may not be paying attention or actually know anything about the subject at hand. How deep your real intelligence goes is not determined solely by the Gemini Ascendant. Possessing a wide spectrum of orientations and abilities, you could be an excellent teacher, writer, scholar or researcher, although the flip-side of this is an inclination towards imitation, plagiarism or even being a con artist.

Manually dexterous, you are not just clever with your hands but have significant artistic and design skills. Lungs and hands are the physically vulnerable areas, while respiratory illnesses and injuries to hands and fingers are common.

 CANCER Rising: Nurturing and tends to be overly sensitive to what they perceive as criticisms.

Cancer Rising makes you ambitious and dedicated, but deceptively vulnerable. You are cautious and not inclined to make the first move until you are sure of your ground. Unfortunately, you seem to attract unsuitable partners and may even be subject to a somewhat traumatic marriage. Your tendency is to marry late in life, and to seek older or more mature partners, or those who represent an authority figure.

You view everything through an emotional glaze, my dears and though you try to hide your vulnerability behind a tough front, this does not fool anyone for long. Be that as it may, you do not usually allow emotional vulnerability to interfere with your ambitions and you have considerable personal magnetism. That emotional commitment makes you work twice as hard as anyone else and generally leads to success. You love to spend time at home and could be successful in any home-based enterprise.

Ruled by the silvery moon, you have a changeable personality, although you can be quite caring and sympathetic when your nurturing instincts are stimulated. You like to be "mothered" and may be guided in life by a strong person (usually female). Consciously or subconsciously you respond to the influence of others, even adopting the latest fashions or modes of behavior whether or not they really suit you or express your deeper character. A tendency to undertake those activities, or studies which appear to improve social standing should be carefully watched, especially when these activities are not actually enjoyable in themselves, nor in keeping with your real inclinations. You are instinctively good with the public and have an affinity with children.

You are a natural cook, and possess strong design or architectural ability, or at least take great interest in them. Roundness of face, pale, sensitive skin, and baldness or finely textured hair are characteristics of Cancer Rising. The body has a strong tendency to retain water, and your emotional orientation (water = emotion) reveals an addictive nature. You seem to attract excess weight - and addictive substances. You can even be addicted to people. Breasts, stomach, and digestive system are vulnerable area

 LEO Rising: Have a "sunny disposition" and tends to be very flirtatious, exhibit strong leadership.

Leo Rising can give you a strong physique and lots of physical stamina. You can be very stubborn and find it extremely difficult to break undesirable habits and behavior patterns. However, this same tenacity and stamina can also be a wonderful asset. When you get involved in something, you hang on long after everyone else runs out of steam, and you inspire others with your devotion to ideals and principles.

Leo has loads of energy and enthusiasm, so, once motivated, you seldom hesitate to act. In spite of all this energy and enthusiasm, the Big Cat can be downright lazy at times. A natural enthusiasm inclines to overabundance and the tendency to overestimate everything. When buying various personal items, for example, you usually acquire far more than you need. Though often rash and hasty, your passions are sincere.

Leo is ruled by the sun, lord of willpower and egotistical drives. Your conscious or subconscious need to dominate means you want the last word in everything, and may come to believe your opinion is the only one worth considering. The negative potential for Leo Ascendant comes out in those whose ego-driven personalities turn them into manipulative, power-oriented demagogues. Though generally outgoing, you are not necessarily aggressive or loudly gregarious. Your personality will be greatly influenced by the nature and strength of your willpower and ego involvement (that is, the placement of your sun and whether it is strengthened by sign and aspect). If the willpower and ego are not strong, then neither is the personality apt to be assertive.

No matter how the rest of the world may see you, it is meaningless compared to how you see yourself. Intense self-absorption makes it hard to accept guidance from others, and you may feel taking or asking for advice is a sign of weakness. You most enjoy associating with those who allow you to shine. Your flamboyant generosity and warm, friendly approach wins many friends, as well as arousing the envy of those with less popular personalities. Life with you is anything but routine.

Your natural creativity gives special talent or ability in art, music, or the entertainment and communication industries. Overwork, anxiety, heart problems, lower back pains, and ailments connected with overindulgence are the most likely physical complaints.

 VIRGO RISING: Tends to be shy at first, always wanting to look at their best, very organized.

Virgo Rising has the ability to adapt to changing circumstances and different people. Your willingness to adapt however, is invariably accompanied by a word or two of complaint. Nowhere is the critical facility associated with Virgo more observable than when this sign rules the Ascendant.

Always seeking perfection, you find it difficult to accept situations or people as they are. You must learn to be more sensitive, my dear, and restrict your passion for constantly finding fault, for even well-meaning criticism can be hurtful and badly received. Practicality and conservatism feature strongly in your personality. While you do not favor flamboyant displays of affection and can even present an excessively puritanical facade in public, you can nevertheless be quite sensual and sexually-oriented in private.

You can be totally organized and attentive to details in some areas, while at the same time be appallingly disorganized and sloppy in other areas. How confusing. How contrary! You are health conscious to the point of obsession and should your natal sun or moon be in one of the Water signs (Cancer, Scorpio, or Pisces) or in Capricorn (which tends toward excessive worry), this concern with health can develop into severe hypochondria.

Ruled by Mercury, the messenger of the gods, you are extremely talkative and prone to gossip. Endlessly curious about everything that goes on in your immediate environment, at times you seem to be everywhere at once. Ideas and projects to take up every waking moment. The knack for collecting and communicating your ideas and information effortlessly attracts information and news from everyone else as well. You readily absorb stores of information which you are happy to share with anyone who takes the time to listen.

Virgo rising gives a talent for communication and attention to detail that makes super salesmen, efficient negotiators, and eager travelers. You like to keep busy and useful. You are nosy, so you would make a great researcher or journalist. Sitting around doing nothing makes you nervous and irritable, but you enjoy collecting such things as recipes, postage stamps, or medical remedies. Respiratory illnesses, nervousness, and allergies are apt to be common physical complaints.

 **LIBRA RISING:** Tends to be attractive in appearance and tends to be a people pleaser.

Libra Rising gives you an energetic, success-oriented personality, so you are dedicated to putting your best foot forward. You are charming and unfailingly polite, although others may sometimes fail to recognize your sincerity. Insensitive types do not realize that you genuinely feel most comfortable and are able to function successfully in a more harmonious environment, rather than hiding behind false manners and charming smiles.

Libra Rising implies a distinct mental orientation. Expressions and mannerisms can give a scholarly appearance, even if you are not particularly learned. You are indeed fond of books, music, or art and though you may seem emotionally detached, your disposition is friendly and eagerly cooperative. However, should something in your physical or mental environment be off balance, you can become cross, demanding, or even tyrannical, until you manage to restore your personal equilibrium.

Libra is ruled by Venus, planet of sensuality and beauty, so you are fortunate enough to be physically attractive. Even if you are not thought of as being physically beautiful, that charming personality will enhance your actual appearance. You are fond of personal luxuries, physical comfort, dressing well, and enhancing your appearance with cosmetics and other beauty aids.

Venus is the planet of romance and sociability, so you are romantic, charming, and gracious. You may have a strong spirit of co-operation and diplomacy, but not necessarily the Libran ability for strategic planning and organization. The negative potential of a Libran ascendant includes the possibility of individuals who are shy, rude or antisocial. It also can mean individuals with either total disregard for their appearance, or the reverse, a vain obsession with retaining youth and beauty at all costs.

You have a definite appreciation for the arts and may be artistically or musically skilled. Interior design, architecture and the law are other areas in which you may take particular interest. You are just as good at taking photographs as you are at posing for them. Common physical complaints are apt to be lack of energy, and ailments that result from addiction to rich foods, particularly sweets.

 SCORPIO RISING: Tends to be secretive about themselves but will act as the "Inquisitor" when they first meet. They tend to make quick appraisals of others.

Scorpio Rising gives you a strong physique and tremendous physical stamina. Far more stubborn than you seem on the surface, you assiduously stick to your goals as long as there is a chance they will be achieved. It is difficult to convince you to change your mind once a decision has been made.

Your emotional vulnerability remains concealed unless your natal sun or moon happens to be in Cancer or Pisces. You are friendly and while you can be rather quiet, you have quite a gregarious personality and don't mind being in the spotlight. It is highly unlikely that you, as a Scorpio rising, have that sinister or mysterious personality which popular literature tends to associate with the sign of Scorpio, but you are a keen observer and a shrewd speculator.

Scorpio is ruled by Pluto, the transformer, and Mars, the warrior. Both planetary influences may be seen in your personality. Ambitious, energetic, you seek activities that are economically rewarding, as well as mentally or physically challenging. The jealousy associated with Mars and Pluto is minimal unless other factors in the chart support such a trait (say Scorpio, Aries or Capricorn Sun). You possess the cleverness and mechanical ability associated with Mars, as well as the innate resourcefulness associated with Pluto. Attracted to others with strong, magnetic personalities, you are oriented toward gathering resources of all kinds. For example, you consciously or subconsciously tend to establish relationships with strong or powerful people in the belief such contacts may prove useful in some way. You can be quite secretive about personal affairs, a trait that often escapes the attention of most people you meet. You are so accommodating and pleasant that, unless others make serious attempts to probe beneath the surface, your real personality and activities may stay hidden indefinitely.

You have remarkable recuperative powers that allow you to recover from physical, mental or economic adversities that would destroy many others. When properly focused, your energy is formidable and you quietly keep going long after everyone else runs out of steam. A Scorpio Ascendant indicates potential for afflictions to the head and face as well as illnesses affecting the reproductive organs.

 SAGITTARIUS RISING: A happy outlook, energetic and optimistic about life.

A Sagittarius Ascendant endows you with the type of flexible personality that works well for you. Because of your need for independence and freedom, you tend to find yourself in changing circumstances and different environments. Such changes of course require a certain amount of adaptability. With a Sagittarian ascendant, you are inclined to put marriage off until later in life (or skip it altogether) unless you find an understanding partner who does not attempt to be possessive or confine you. Once such an acceptable marriage arrangement is made however, the Archer adapts and makes a stable, loyal spouse.

You are full of energetic enthusiasm. However, your enthusiasm is not always accompanied by unflagging physical energy. You may, in fact, tend to be lazy unless highly motivated to perform. It is often difficult to engage in boring routine exercise and in spite of your innate restlessness and propensity for rushing around in a myriad of activities, you are quite capable of being unwilling (or unable) to keep yourself trim and in good physical shape. Though often rash and hasty, your passions are sincere and inspirational.

Sagittarius is ruled by Jupiter, planet of inspiration, wisdom, good fortune, and abundance. You are inclined to be spiritually or philosophically oriented, talkative, intellectually curious, and, at times, perhaps a bit too impressed with status and wealth. Your natural exuberance and generosity are responsible for unrestrained abundance. Like those with Gemini rising, you are apt to demonstrate any one of a wide range of orientations and abilities: from being a great teacher, writer, scholar or researcher, all the way down to engaging in the flimflam of con artistry and the intellectual emptiness of copying the originality and talent of others.

You are usually very honest, though it is also true that your too-candid remarks can sometimes be misinterpreted as rudeness. Negative influences associated with Sagittarius rising stimulate a tendency for self-indulgence, which makes you pompous, grossly overweight, dependent on drugs or alcohol, or too opinionated and cynical. On the positive side, Sagittarius gives a love of drama and the theatre, good food and drink, dancing, sports, animals, and, as a rule, you'll never miss an opportunity to travel. You are likely to be involved with publishing, education, religion, art, or music, either as a profession or hobby.

CAPRICORN RISING: Will be very traditional and want to look successful.

Capricorn Rising endows an energetic, success-oriented personality, with the determination to achieve your personal goals. The shrewdness and open ambition associated with the sun or moon in Capricorn does not always show up so overtly in the personality of those with Capricorn Ascendant but these traits are present nevertheless. You could be a very capable manager or supervisor, willing to accept responsibilities and positions of authority.

You strongly identify with the material world and tangible assets. You are unlikely to adopt easy-going, "take me as I am" attitudes, for you feel more comfortable with formality. You want to be aware of all the rules of social conduct and adapt your actions to fit these structures. Consciously or subconsciously you specifically choose the company of people who make you look good. It is not unusual for handsome Capricorn Rising males to select less attractive wives or, beautiful Capricorn Rising women to select less attractive female friends.

Ruled by Saturn, lord of structure, restriction and longevity, you may have experienced a difficult birth or restricted childhood. However, it hardly matters what particular difficulties life presents you with, for your biggest challenge is always you in yourself. You feel dissatisfaction with some aspect of your personality or appearance and may develop conflicting behavior to deal with these feelings when they surface. One side of your character is prone to practice strict self denial, while the other longs to abandon itself to hedonistic pleasures, perhaps as a form of self destruction. At every turn you confront fears and insecurity. How well you deal with the conflict marks your success as a well-adjusted adult. Fortunately, these conflicts seem to settle into perspective as you get older.

Capricorn ruling the first house raises the competitive spirit and by no means dictates the presence of a somber or colorless personality. On the contrary, it implies individuals with overly compensating cheerful personalities, who willingly accept responsibilities and hardships which they feel they were born to endure. There is always a choice to be made and the right one is never easy, because it usually involves success which must be earned.

Your abstemious eating habits help you avoid gaining too much weight. Sensitive skin, finely textured hair, brittle bones, and dental difficulties are common physical complaints.

AQUARIUS RISING: Will be very friendly or can appear to be aloof or other wise preoccupied. These people will try to be "different" than others, can be "quirky", always a surprise!

Aquarius Rising gives you a detached, intellectual outlook, combined with considerable mental poise. You stay cool under pressure and take sudden shocks or unexpected changes in your stride. An interest, not to say a fascination with the bizarre and unusual can lead you down some rather interesting pathways. Status, power, and wealth are of marginal value, for you are interested in people for their own sake, not the social trappings which accompany them. Friendships are easily made and not so easily broken, for your air of easygoing familiarity and pleasant demeanor is rather attractive.
Ruled by Uranus (lord of reversals and unexpected upheavals) and Saturn, lord of karma (purification and restriction), your personality can be changeable, yet deeply focused and quite original in approach. Most likely your life will undergo one or more dramatic changes of direction, often through some twist of fate or circumstances over which you have no control. Changes can occur suddenly and unexpectedly, for though Saturn's influence implies a calm and stable disposition, Uranus often reacts in quite unexpected ways. Unpredictable and independent, you can be argumentative and love to play devil's advocate. You need your personal freedom, so when you marry or form partnerships you should choose your partners with care, since you are quite unable to put up with possessiveness and over-dependence. You enjoy physical and mental stimulation and, my dears, whilst you are keenly interested in the future and are fascinated by the past (especially the offbeat, little-known areas), you somehow lose track of what's going on in the present. Ahead of your time, others may perceive you as out of step with the rest of society.

Your strong physique and reserves of stamina, combined with your notorious stubbornness makes it difficult to break undesirable habits and behavior patterns. Your independence is legendary and, of course, you do tend to be somewhat opinionated, especially in matters that have stimulated your interest in the offbeat.

Others stand little chance of changing your ideas, for you must become convinced on your own account that such changes are necessary. You probably like science, sociology, music and design, while your pursuit of hidden things and unusual research can lead you to an interest in astrology and other arcane matters. You are good with money, which tends to come your way unexpectedly, yet appropriately to your lifestyle. You are subject to nervous conditions, problems with the lower legs, ankles and stiffness or inflexibility of the bones and joints.

 PISCES RISING: Very nurturing, dreamy and people never seem to see you as the same person. You may have "watery eyes".

Pisces Rising gives a flexible personality, with which you can easily hide your own traits and take on the characteristics of others. Despite your pleasant disposition and willingness to adapt to changing circumstance and the demands of other people, you can be surprisingly strong and determined. The strength of your character, however, is also determined by other important factors in your background.

You have a highly emotional nature, with a quiet, shy personality. Compassionate feelings can be overwhelming, and you must watch the tendency to become a victim of your own vulnerability. Almost before you realize it, or in some cases because you actually seek it, you become your own worst enemy. You are not above using subterfuge and game-playing rather than direct confrontation to get what you want. If however, you develop self-confidence, these less-than-honest emotional ploys are not apt to surface in your personality or behavior patterns.

Pisces is ruled by Neptune, lord of illusion and imagination, so you have little understanding of how you appear to others. The influence of Neptune can also add an element of glamour or mystery to your appearance. You can for example, either photograph extremely well or your likeness on film may be extremely poor. In either case, photographs fail to capture your true appearance. Pisces is also ruled by Jupiter, lord of inspiration and drama. Neptune and Jupiter blend together to create a highly imaginative personality and one which views life the way you want it to be, rather than the way it really is. Prone to feelings of abandonment, you often feel sorry for yourself and are easily disillusioned.

Your extreme sensitivity generates artistic or poetic talent as well as psychic abilities. Pisces endows a spiritual or philosophical bent, and great appreciation for education, even should your own have been limited. You love traveling, dancing, and sports and although it is by no means universal with Pisces Rising, you may be less-than-average in physical stature with a tendency to retain fluids. An addictive nature makes you extremely vulnerable to habit-forming substances. Sensitivity to medicine and anesthesia and problems with the feet are typical physical complaints.

My RISING SIGN IS:_____.

I would say this about myself when it comes to how I tend to view the world: _____

_____
_____
_____.

When first meeting me, other people have commented to me that I appear to be

_____
_____
_____
_____.

As I grow and understand myself more, I would say that I am trying to aspire to be more like

_____
_____
_____.

How to Determine Your Rising Sign

To find your true Rising Sign, you need to have your birth chart calculated by an Astrologer, but you can estimate yourself, without complex Calculations, by this chart, if you know your birth time.

SUN Sign	ARIES	TAURUS	GEMINI	CANCER	LEO	VIRGO	LIBRA	SCOR-PIO	SAG	CAP	AQU	PISCES
6AM-8AM	Aries	Taurus	Gemini	Cancer	Leo	Virgo	Libra	Scorpio	Sag	Capricorn	Aquarius	Pisces
4AM-6AM	Pisces	Aries	Taurus	Gemini	Cancer	Leo	Virgo	Libra	Scorpio	Sag	Capricorn	Aquarius
2AM-4AM	Aquarius	Pisces	Aries	Taurus	Gemini	Cancer	Leo	Virgo	Libra	Scorpio	Sag	Capricorn
MID-2AM	Capricorn	Aquarius	Pisces	Aries	Taurus	Gemini	Cancer	Leo	Virgo	Libra	Scorpio	Sag
10PM-MID	Sagittarius	Capricorn	Aquarius	Pisces	Aries	Taurus	Gemini	Cancer	Leo	Virgo	Libra	Scorpio
8PM-10PM	Scorpio	Sag	Capricorn	Aquarius	Pisces	Aries	Taurus	Gemini	Cancer	Leo	Virgo	Libra
6PM-8PM	Libra	Scorpio	Sag	Capricorn	Aquarius	Pisces	Aries	Taurus	Gemini	Cancer	Leo	Virgo
4PM-6PM	Virgo	Libra	Scorpio	Sag	Capricorn	Aquarius	Pisces	Aries	Taurus	Gemini	Cancer	Leo
2PM-4PM	Leo	Virgo	Libra	Scorpio	Sag	Capricorn	Aquarius	Pisces	Aries	Taurus	Gemini	Cancer
NOON-2PM	Cancer	Leo	Virgo	Libra	Scorpio	Sag	Capricorn	Aquarius	Pisces	Aries	Taurus	Gemini
10AM-NOON	Gemini	Cancer	Leo	Virgo	Libra	Scorpio	Sag	Capricorn	Aquarius	Pisces	Aries	Taurus
8AM-10AM	Taurus	Gemini	Cancer	Leo	Virgo	Libra	Scorpio	Sag	Capricorn	Aquarius	Pisces	Aries

The Moon's Nodes ~ North and South

Most astrologers consider the Nodes to have the same level of importance as the Sun, Moon and other visible planets, and history does show that the movement of the Nodes has a very significant effect on our destinies. These points are also used to interpret past life experiences or relationships as well as our present life purpose. The symbol looks like a horseshoe. The only difference in the symbol is that the horseshoe is open on the bottom for the north node ☊ and open on the top for the south node . ☋

The nodes are not physical bodies but actual points in space. They are points in the heavens where the intersection of the Moon's orbit with the plane of the ecliptic (the path of the Sun and planets as they appear to revolve around the earth) take place. The north or ascending node shows where the Moon crosses the Sun's path from south to north. The south or descending node is formed when the Moon travels from a northerly to southerly celestial latitude. In Chinese astrology, 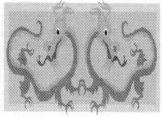 the nodes are referred to as the dragon's head (north node) and the dragon's tail (south node). The Nodes travel backwards at approximately 3' per day. It takes approximately 18 years for a full cycle of the lunar nodes. When the Sun and Moon are in conjunction, and either lunar node is also in conjunction with both, a solar eclipse occurs. When the Sun and Moon are in opposition, and each is in conjunction with one of the lunar nodes, a lunar eclipse occurs. Eclipses occur when the new or full moon occurs within 12 degrees of a node within 5 degrees for a Total Eclipse).

 Philosophically speaking... In the birth chart, **The Dragon's Head (North Node)** represents the future and those things we are trying to attain in this lifetime, as well as new learning experiences we need to aspire towards, which will ultimately lead to our personal growth. In other words... it's what we were put on this earth to do.

 The Dragon's Tail (South Node), which lies directly opposite the North Node in our chart, represents knowledge we bring from our past and our inborn talents, or abilities and is often expressed at an early age. Because the South Node functioning seems so natural, easy, and comfortable, we can get stuck there. Eventually we may become bored, limited, stunted in our growth, and depleted of energy.

For the polarity to remain balanced, both sides must be equally represented, otherwise we can remain fixated in the South Node's realm and avoid the path of future development depicted by the North Node's sign and house position.

On the next pages we will be looking at the house and sign positions of your North and South Nodes, in order to determine what your inherent strengths are and what your life purpose would be more beneficially directed towards.

Lunar Nodes by the Signs
Andrew M. Riley www.lunarnodes.co.uk

Aries Taurus Gemini Cancer Leo Virgo Libra Scorpio Sagittarius Capricorn Aquarius Pisces

North Node in Aries: There is a need for the person to display independence and to learn to operate on their own initiative. They are more likely to succeed with the support of those who are self-confident and daring. **South Node in Libra:** The individual has learnt to be decisive and not dependent on others, they can also operate well during periods of upheaval and great change.

North Node in Taurus: There is a need for the person to be self-sufficient and self-reliant in this life. They are more likely to succeed if seek those who can help by providing security and stability so the person has a peaceful and harmonious base to build on. **South Node in Scorpio:** The individual has learnt not to be controlled by others and needs to avoid intense and, potentially, traumatic situations.

North Node in Gemini: There is a need for the person to communicate and pass on their skills, talents or knowledge to others. They are innate teachers and learners and need the support and interaction with people that are intelligent and good communicators. **South Node in Sagittarius:** The individual has learnt not to be over-confident and to curb their compulsion to travel.

North Node in Cancer: There is a need for the person to become involved in the care of others. They are more likely to succeed if they gain the support of those that can provide mutual care and nurturing.

South Node in Capricorn: The individual has learnt not to be over-ambitious and not to rely on their accomplishments or reputation.

North Node in Leo: There is a need for the person to display both creativity and discipline in their life, they need an organized base on which they can build. They are more likely to succeed if they have the support of people with outgoing personalities who are not afraid to be in the public arena.

South Node in Aquarius: The individual has learnt to tread the fine line between genius and outspoken defiance.

North Node in Virgo: There is a need for the person to be selfless and be of service to others. They are more likely to succeed with the support of hard working and conscientious friends. **South Node in Pisces**: The individual has learnt to be realistic and not get carried away by dreams and fantasy.

North Node in Libra: There is a need for the person to recognize the value of sharing, being an equal with others in life rather than taking the limelight. They are more likely to succeed if they seek people who can help to provide peace and harmony. **South Node in Aries:** The individual has learnt not to be selfish, thinking of themselves before others, or being irresponsible.

North Node in Scorpio: There is a need for the person to transform and regenerate their lives and accept the tremendous changes that are in store. They are more likely to succeed with the support of people with powerful magnetism and charisma. **South Node in Taurus**: The individual has learnt not to be thinking always of themselves and be supportive and flexible with others.

North Node in Sagittarius: There is a need for the person to be honest and learn the value of good judgment and discernment. They are more likely to succeed with the support of people who will act as a teacher and are likely to learn great things off people from foreign lands or cultures. **South Node in Gemini:** The individual has learnt not to gossip and be too voluble (to the point of boring people). They are not concerned by the minutiae of everyday life.

North Node in Capricorn: There is a need for the person to work hard in this life to achieve their ambitions. They are more likely to succeed if they seek the support of those that know the value of the long slow road to the top (rather than the faster drop over the cliff!). **South Node in Cancer**: The individual has learnt to overcome the painful links or restrictions with the past despite opposition or interference from the family.

North Node in Aquarius: There is a need for the person to be more integrated, playing his part in society and to contribute as a member of a team. They are more likely to succeed with the support of those who can help in making contacts within the community or show a high level of inventiveness or resourcefulness. **South Node in Leo:** The individual has learnt to take life seriously and not to treat it as a game only for them to play.

North Node in Pisces: There is a need for the person to seek the peace and harmony of a more spiritual path to give their life meaning. They are more likely to succeed with the support of those that can act as spiritual guides and give the person a more sacred objectivity. **South Node in Virgo:** The individual has learnt that there is more to life than compulsive perfection and a routine born of obsession.

(North Node in 1st House/South Node in 7th House) North: There is a need for the person to become more assertive and impose their will to succeed. The individuals are more likely to need acquaintances who demonstrate independence or bravery in their field. **South:** This position indicates a willingness to work independently of partners. Lovers were key influences in previous lives and so there is little need for that sort of dependency during this life.

(North Node in 2nd House/South Node in 8th House) North: There is a need for the person to achieve stability and security in their life. The individuals are more likely to need the assistance of those who can provide the comfort of financial support and well being. **South:** This position indicates that the individual has thrown off the shackles of those that would seek to abuse their power over the person. The individual has also learnt that it is possible to succeed without resorting to extreme or dangerous actions.

(North Node in 3rd House/South Node in 9th House) North: There is a need for the person to be integrated and accepted into the community. The individual is more likely to need the assistance of those that would provide the necessary contacts in the community. Alternatively, they may require help from brothers or sisters and contacts from the world of communication and travel. **South:** This position indicates that the individual has learnt to control their itchy feet and not need to travel to widen their experience. They also have no need for outdated belief systems or philosophies.

(North Node in 4th House/South Node in 10th House) North: There is a need for the person to place the focus firmly on family affairs despite outside influences. Family members or people with links to the past are essential factors in helping the individual to succeed in this life. **South:** The individual has learnt to live without the need for praise or recognition. They can now succeed without seeking plaudits from their contemporaries.

(North Node in 5th House/South Node in 11th House) North: There is a need for the person to be creative in order to succeed in this life. They will obtain great value from learning to play and the influence of children will be formative in their success. **South:** The individual has learnt to become independent of politics or the influence of friends. Similarly, they have no need for the social niceties and the support of the community in their work.

(North Node in 6th House/South Node in 12th House) North: There is a need for the person to learn the value of hard work and a healthy lifestyle. They are more likely to succeed with the assistance of their peers in their chosen profession. They will also need the help of people with an eye for detail. **South:** The individual has learnt to live realistically and shun the world of fantasy and escapism.

(North Node in 7th House/South Node in 1st House) North: There is a need for the person to develop their intimate relationships as a focus to success in this life. They are unlikely to succeed if there is no mutual attraction between their partners in life and love. **South:** The individual has learnt to accept the assistance of others and not to plough a lonely, solitary furrow.

(North Node in 8th House/South Node in 2nd House) North: There is a need for the person to accept the unorthodox, to actively seek the unknown and the means to impose your own power on life. They are more likely to succeed if they seek the assistance of those with a powerful magnetism that will transform or regenerate their life. These people are also likely to need the partnership of people with equally powerful sexuality and emotions. **South:** The individual has overcome a feeling of inadequacy through the development of an innate sense of well-being and personal security.

(North Node in 9th House/South Node in 3rd House) North: There is a need for the person to pursue their own spiritual path and synthesize their own individual philosophy. They are more likely to succeed if they seek spiritual mentors in this life, whether they be teachers or advisors, foreigners or even animal guides. **South:** The individual has learnt to overcome the minutiae of everyday life and become independent of the influences from their brother or sister.

(North Node in 10th House/South Node in 4th House) North: There is a need for the person to build and impose their reputation within and on society. They are unlikely to succeed without the support of those that can build their confidence and enable them to achieve their objectives. **South:** The individual has learnt to overcome the painful links or restrictions with the past despite opposition or interference from the family.

(North Node in 11th House/South Node in 5th House) North: There is a need for the person to be more integrated, playing his part in society and to contribute as a member of a team. They are more likely to succeed with the support of those who can help in making contacts within the community or show a high level of inventiveness or resourcefulness. **South:** The individual has learnt to take life seriously and not to treat it as a game only for them to play.

(North Node in 12th House/South Node in 6th House) North: There is a need for the person to seek the peace and harmony of a more spiritual path to give their life meaning. They are more likely to succeed with the support of those that can act as spiritual guides and give the person a more sacred objectivity. **South:** The individual has learnt that there is more to life than compulsive perfection and a routine born of obsession.

 My NORTH NODE is in the sign of _____.

It is in my _____HOUSE. This tells me that my path or goals in life are to
_____
_____
_____
_____

 My SOUTH NODE is in the sign of _____.

It is in my _____ HOUSE. This tells me that I am trying to leave behind
my need for (to)
_____
_____
_____
_____.

NOW....Create YOUR chart!

1. Put in the House numbers
2. Put in your RISING Sign
3. Add the PLANETS & the SIGN they are in
4. Mark the PLANETS that are Rx
5. Add the NORTH & SOUTH NODES & SiGNS they are in.

Practice makes perfect!

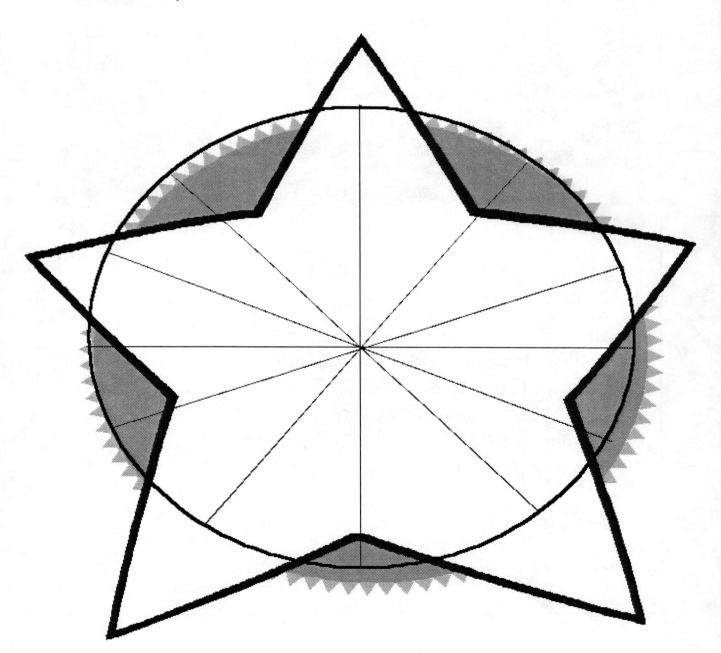

Chapter 4

1.   RETROGRADE Planets
2.   Planets & ASPECTS
3.   Exercise: Drawing Aspects
4.   Astrological GLOSSARY of TERMS

Retrograde (Rx) Planets

All of the planets go Retrograde (Rx) during the year. The planets aren't actually going retrograde, or backwards, but they slow down in their heavenly movement and appear to be going backwards...or retrograde. When the planet Mercury does this 4 times a year, for approximately 3 weeks, we seem to notice the effects more.   Following is a list of words to help explain the types of activities that are most suited during Retrograde activity:

~reach ~ react ~ reacquire ~ readapt ~ readdress ~ readjourn ~ readmit ~ readopt ~ ready ~ **reaffirm** ~ realistic ~ **realize** ~ reannex ~ reappear ~ **reapply** ~ reappoint ~ reapportion ~ reargue ~reason ~ reassemble ~ reassume ~ reattach ~ reattack ~ reavow ~ rebate ~ rebel ~ rebirth ~ rebloom ~ reboil ~ rebound ~ rebroadcast ~ rebuff ~ rebut ~ rebuild ~ rebuke ~ rebury ~ recall ~ recant ~ recapitulate ~ recapture ~ recelebrate ~ recede ~ **receive** ~ rechallenge ~ recharge ~ recharter ~ recheck ~ rechoose ~ reclasp ~ reclean ~ reclothe ~ recognize ~ recoil ~ recollect ~ recoin ~ recolonize ~ recolor ~ recombine ~ recommence ~ recommission ~ recompense ~ **reconcile** ~ reconduct ~ reconnoiter ~ reconquer ~ reconsecrate ~ **reconsider** ~ reconstruct ~ reconsolidate ~ reconvene ~ **recopy** ~ record ~ recounter ~ recoup ~ recourse ~ **recover** ~ recreate ~ recriminate ~ rectify ~ recruit ~ recuperate ~ recur ~ recrystallize ~ recultivate ~ rededicate ~ redeem ~ redefeat ~ redefine ~ redeposit ~ redetermine ~ redigest ~ **rediscover** ~ redissolve ~ redistill ~ redistribute ~ redivide ~ **redo** ~ redraw ~ reduce ~ redye ~ reecho ~ reedit ~ reelect ~ reelevate ~ **reembark** ~ reembody ~ reembrace ~ reemerge ~ reemigrate ~ reenact ~ reendow ~ reinforce ~ reengage ~ rekindle ~ reenlist ~ reenter ~ reestablish ~ **reevaluate** ~ reexamine ~ reexchange ~ reexperience ~ reexport ~ reface ~ refashion ~ refasten ~ refertilize ~ refile ~ **refine** ~ refire ~ reflect ~ reflex ~ reflower ~ refold ~ reforge ~ reform ~ reformulate ~ refortify ~ refract ~ reframe ~ refreeze ~ **refresh** ~ refuel ~ refund ~ refurbish ~ refurnish~ refuse ~ refute ~ regale ~ regard ~ regenerate ~ regerminate ~ regild ~ regurgitate ~ reglaze ~ reglue ~ regrade ~ regraft ~ **regroup** ~ rehabilitate ~ rehandle ~ rehear ~ reheat ~ reheel ~ rehire ~ reignite ~ reimburse ~ reimpose ~ reimpregnate ~ reimpress ~ reimprint ~ reinaugurate ~ reincite ~ reincorporate ~ reincur ~ reinduce ~ reinfect ~ reinflame ~ reinfuse ~ reinhabit ~ reinoculate ~ reinsert ~ reinspect ~ reinspire ~ reinstall ~ reinstruct ~ reintegrate ~ reinterrogate ~ reintrench ~ reintroduce ~ **reinvent** ~ reinvest ~ **reinvestigate** ~ reinvigorate ~ reinvite ~ reinvolve ~ rejudge ~ rekindle ~ relabel ~ **replace** ~ relate ~ **relax** ~ relay ~ **release** ~ relegate ~ relent ~ relieve ~ relinquish ~ relaunch ~ relaunder ~ relearn ~ relight~ reliquidate ~ relive ~ reload ~ relocate ~ remake ~ remanufacture ~ remain ~ remarry ~ remeasure ~ remelt ~ **reemerge** ~ remix ~ ~ **remodify** ~ remold ~ rename ~ renavigate ~ renege ~ renominate ~ renotify ~ renounce ~ renovate ~ renumber ~ renunciate ~ reobtain ~ reoccupy ~ reoccur ~ reopen ~ reoppose ~ reordain ~ repacify ~ repack ~ repaint ~ repair ~ repaper ~ repave ~ repeat ~ repenalize ~ **replace** ~ replant ~ replay ~ repledge ~ replenish ~ reply ~ report ~ repose ~ repolish ~ repopulate ~ repour ~ represent ~ repress ~ reprieve ~ reproach ~ **reproduce** ~ reprocess ~ reproclaim ~ **republish** ~ repudiate ~ repulse ~ repurchase ~ repurify ~ repurge ~ reread ~ rerecord ~ reroll ~ reroute ~ rerun ~ reseal ~ reseed ~ reserve ~ reset ~ respect ~ respond ~ **rest** ~ restate ~ restock ~ restore ~ restrain ~ **resume** ~ resurge ~ resurrect ~ retaliate ~ reticent ~ retire ~ retort ~ retouch ~ retrace ~ retread ~ **retreat** ~ retrench ~ retrial ~ retrieve ~ return ~ **reunite** ~ reveal ~ revel ~ reengage ~ revere ~ reverse ~ review ~ revise ~ revive ~ revoke ~ revolt ~ revolve ~ **reward** ~ rework ~ rewrite

All About RETROGRADE Planets

Retrograde (Rx) planets in a chart seem to mean that one is conditioned to being held back; that one tends to accept limitation and having to take the long way around, that one must adjust to the indirect approach and having to work harder for what one wants in life. When these planets turn up in your chart, these attributes can be lifelong, even becoming more ingrained as the years go by, and can sometimes be traced back to early childhood circumstances.

It is wise to recognize that these can be blessings in disguise, as these planets tend to work more on the inner plane and can signify greater opportunity for growth and attainment through tapping into one's inner resources. The Rx position always gives the individual the power to go back again and regain something. It is much like sweeping a room with a broom, going back and forth until you get it right. A Rx planet brings success only after all else has failed, thereby giving these planets more of a spiritual nature than material consideration.

MERCURY Rx: The planet Mercury is retrograde (Rx) 4 times a year for approximately 3 weeks. While Mercury is Rx, we can expect to have many changes and disruptions in matters dealing with communications: letters, telephone calls, faxes, e-mails; machines & travel. This is an excellent time to do additional research, to reconsider plans and to reexamine your resources. People and projects from the past may reenter our lives. It is highly recommended that you avoid purchasing new items or beginning new projects during this time if you can. It is important to pay more attention to the details during this period...or you may find yourself redoing things more than once! Those of you who are ruled by the planet Mercury, or who have strong Mercury aspects may be more bothered by this than others.

Mercury Rx natives may find that their minds function more easily on the subconscious level, they tend to talk to themselves and do not always seem to hear what people say to them.

My Mercury is_____ is not _____ Retrograde (Rx)

VENUS Rx: This aspect in a chart can mean that an old love affair could be rekindled or money earned from the past may suddenly turn up. People born with Venus Rx are sometimes inclined towards unconventional love affairs, or they may denounce love entirely and retreat into a more monastic existence. The creative urge can be quite intense. Artists, musicians, poets, dress designers and dancers frequently have Venus Rx. Oftentimes their talents go unnoticed until a succeeding generation recognizes their genius. The real motivation of Venus Rx is the exposure of sham. These people are quite sensitive to what is phony and they can be quite blunt about what they see or feel!

My Venus is_____ is not _____Retrograde (Rx)

MARS Rx: While this planet is RX, one might find that their physical energy is just not up to par, and that rest is more of a requirement. If you are born with this placement, your physical energy and vitality may only kick in when it is triggered by some subconscious motivation, completely unrelated to the act itself. With Mars (the planet of action) Rx, it can imply a stubborn, unyielding physical force which does not move until some mystical reason is found for its expression. It can indicate impotence or frigidity. These people often make good scientists and doctors, or other occupations which require the handling of physical material in an objective, non-involved way. They are very good at planning and organizing the physical labors of others. Physical activity to these people connotes an image of pain or effort, therefore, the frequently rebel against their own desires, try to stifle them, preferring to act, when they have to, against tremendous odds; subconsciously seeking an excuse for the failure they anticipate.

My Mars is _____ is not_____ Retrograde (Rx)

♃ JUPITER Rx: People with Jupiter RX often find success in the failures of others. By starting at the point where others have become discouraged, these people have a unique ability for finding the gold of opportunity in projects which have been abandoned. They usually don't respond with as much enthusiasm for obvious opportunities for gain, but can become animated and alert for profits they can derive from situations which look unpromising to the experts. They can appear to be totally out of step with the times, but because their opportunism is so closely allied to their subconscious intuitive processes, they are usually found to be right. Their subconscious ability to be so flexible to the unknown becomes their key to success.

My JUPITER is_____ is not _____ Retrograde (Rx)

♄ SATURN Rx: While Saturn is Rx, we are advised to really consider our actions and the responsibilities associated with them. Individuals with this aspect in their chart tend to be shy, uneasy or introverted and there is a need to be on guard against subconscious defeatism which can undermine their most noble ambitions. They can have a strong sense of fate which controls their destiny. They may feel alone, isolated and separated form their fellow man at times. These people may cover up feelings of insecurity with a cloak of arrogance or super sophistication, an air of boredom or an impression that nothing shocks them...when in fact they really are shockable. They may find security in intellectual or spiritual havens. When they are in this mode, they adjust to material setbacks with great ease, subconsciously getting to realize that what appears to be real is not...and that passive acceptance can become a positive force when applied to the spiritual realm, attracting the inner security they seek.

My SATURN is_____ is not _____ Retrograde (Rx)

♅ URANUS Rx: With this placement, the motivating factor is unconscious rebellion against the self. These people can be the most creative people imaginable, for they are continually "tilling the soil" of self, uncovering rusty coins which others have discarded and polishing them to discover gold. They may see themselves as being unappreciated. They are trying to constantly find themselves, and never do...but in the process, find so much of value to others. Oftentimes you are at odds with others of your generation, constructing truth which others do not wish to face.

It is possible that in prior times, you experienced great personal instability as a result of impersonal, collective impulses toward change (during a time of revolution, political upheaval, war, etc.). You may well have been an agent of these movements, with a lingering inclination toward radical solutions, extremism, flauntingly disregarding social mores. Or you may have become a reactionary, fearing and resisting all reforms or departures from the "main stream". It is thus difficult for you to be balanced and fair towards any eccentricities (in others or even in yourself). A misuse of science or technology, perhaps participating in experiments, which were harmful to you or others, is also indicated. Thus, you may have a deep distrust of or an attraction/repulsion toward science and technological advancement.

My URANUS is_____ is not _____ Retrograde (Rx)

71

NEPTUNE Rx: People with Neptune Rx is often found in individuals guilty of spiritual inconsistency. They can be unusually psychic, but very skeptical of their extrasensory perceptions. A self-deprecating air I is usually their way of relating to the world...they do not usually suffer from pride. They enjoy seclusion and often will escape from the more material concerns of life.

People with Neptune Rx may have had a prior lifetime or lifetimes in which they dissipated their energy, fell away from their disciplines, or were too passive or irresolute to go after the spiritual opportunities open to them at that time. This carries over as a vague yet persistent inner nagging that you should be further on than you are, or a fear of spiritual failure. You may also have been involved in mystical or magical practices that created distortions in your life. It is important for you to take a balanced, patient, well-grounded attitude toward life - nothing too otherworldly, ethereal, or glamorous. Indulging in any mood-altering substances is particularly deleterious for you.

My NEPTUNE is_____ is not _____ Retrograde (Rx)

PLUTO Rx: People who subconsciously rebel against the force of group pressure usually have this aspect in their charts. These individuals are never sure that they belong in your social environment, nor are they consciously sure that they want to. They are extremely conscious of social caste and we can find both snobs and hobos with Pluto Rx. They will subconsciously ally themselves with either the underdog or the super dog...and they hold the seeds of sainthood or anarchy within them. Secretly, these people desire to change the course of their lives and create an entirely new order for themselves...if only on a small scale. Their actions and reactions, which involve others, need to be carefully and objectively analyzed for the effects they will have up society.

My PLUTO is_____ is not _____ Retrograde (Rx)

Time for a quick review!

I have (#) _____ Rx Planets in my chart.

They are: _____,_____,

_____ , _____,

_____, _____,

_____, _____.

Planets and Aspects

The PLANETS

- Each **planet** symbolizes certain sides of your character. Planets are located symbolically in the chart: the signs and houses filter their energies through the planets, much as a colored lens filters the image thrown by a stage-light, or received by a camera.
- Planets which are particularly expressive of certain signs are said to rule these signs; a planet whose energies are most powerfully channeled through a certain sign is said to be exalted in that sign.
- Planets can have a positive (day) or a negative (night) rulership, but only one exaltation. The symbolism is so carefully designed that a planet placed in the opposite sign to its exaltation is found to be weak in the expression of its natural powers and is said to be in fall; planets in the opposite signs to their rulership are also weakly placed and are said to be in detriment. We will talk more about this in the Intermediate workbook.
- The planet which is most strongly placed in your birth-chart is called your **Ruling Planet.** This is usually the **ruler of the ascendant**, but could be **the ruler of the sign in which the Sun (sun-ruler) or Moon (moon-ruler) is placed**, depending on its strength by sign, aspect and elevation.
- Other powerfully placed planets must also be taken into consideration, for example Mars in Capricorn conjunct the Mid-Heaven, strongly aspected, would be a candidate for rulership, especially should the other rulers mentioned be weak.

ASPECTS

Geometrical relationships between planets are called aspects; these affect the energies of the planets concerned. Should a planet have difficult aspects, or be in an unsympathetic position in the zodiac, it is said to be **afflicted**; its negative characteristics may be exhibited on occasions in your character. Difficult aspects, usually manifest their results in being more conducive to personal development, often generating complex results that require considerable interpretation and self-analysis. More about that later!

Difficult aspects, especially to what can be called   **"malefic" (dangerous) planets**, are often quite problematic and can even be catastrophic in their effects. These aspects tend to generate complex results requiring considerable interpretation and self-analysis, while favorable aspects more often produce simple effects which are easy to understand. In any case, the chart must be always viewed as a whole, for positive and negative characteristics can cancel each other out, or appear in mitigated forms, according to circumstances depending upon other factors.

Should it have **easy or favorable aspects**, its effects may be more beneficial. Favorable aspects more often produce simple effects which are easy to understand. In any case, the chart must be viewed as a whole, for the positive and negative characteristics may cancel out, or appear in mitigated forms, according to circumstances depending upon other factors. always viewed as a whole, for positive and negative characteristics can cancel each other out, or appear in mitigated forms, according to circumstances depending upon other factors.

The MEANINGS of the ASPECTS:

In the past, aspects were considered to be EASY or BENIGN, other aspects were considered to be DIFFICULT or MALEFIC. In today's view, MALEFIC aspects has been changed to CHALLENGING and are considered to be CRISES in ACTION or CONSCIOUSNESS.

Powerful ASPECTS:

CONJUNCTION: (0' - 10') A conjunction seems to increase the energies of all planets involved in the conjunction. The planets involved will work together and are mixed or tied to each other, giving more POWER and FORCE to those energies involved. POSITIVELY it brings a blending and unifying of the energies, NEGATIVELY it can bring an over-emphasis or dependency.

SQUARE: (90') This aspect is one of the most difficult aspects, as it tends to create tension and conflict. It is considered to be very karmic and this is where your lessons will be learned...the hard way! This aspect demands that you do a lot of work before you see any results. POSIITVELY, it can bring incentive and challenges, NEGATIVELY, it can bring conflicts & obstacles.

TRINE (120') This is one of the most easy aspects you can have in your chart. The trine reinforces, amplifies, exaggerates and harmonizes the energies of the planets involved. It is considered to be a gift. Many feel that this aspect represents having mastered certain energies from previous incarnations. It creates ease in the areas it is applied. POSITIVELY, it can bring good fortune and help to facilitate. NEGATIVELY, it can bring indecision and laziness.

OPPOSITION (180') This aspect will create a see-saw effect, similar to the full moon. Its purpose is to bring BALANCE to your experiences through confrontation. You will first be on one side of an issue, then on the other. POSITIVELY, one can experience awareness and balance, NEGATIVELY, it can bring dilemma and indecision.

Moderate ASPECTS:

SEXTILE: (60') This is an "opportunity" aspect and it tends to support, aid or assist us in the transitions in our lives. POSITIVELY, it can bring opportunity and cooperation, NEGATIVELY, it can bring passivity and gullibility.

SESQUIQUADRATE (135'): indicates strain and should be carefully watched if they occur between 2 major planets.

QUINCUNX or INCONJUNCT: (150') This is one of the most overlooked aspects in a chart. It can bring painful transitions in our lives, or relationships, which require painful adjustment. This aspect is halfway between a SQUARE and a TRINE, so it seems to evidence both qualities. POSITIVELY, it can bring adjustments and choice, NEGATIVELY, it can bring struggle and confrontation.

Weak ASPECTS:

SEMI-SEXTILE: (30') The POSITIVE meaning of this aspect is that aptitude is there or assistance will be available, the NEGATIVE meaning can bring unconcern and procrastination.

SEMISQUARE (45') This is a "warning" aspect, as it seems to prepare us for the bigger challenges ahead...the SQUARE aspect. POSITIVELY, it can bring awareness, fore thought and self-control, NEGATIVELY, it can be irritation and feeling as if one is "out of step".

ORBS of Influence:

An ORB describes how close a certain PLANET is to another PLANET. The closer the DEGREE or the closer the ASPECT, the stronger its influence is. Generally speaking, an orb of 1-10 DEGREES is taken when considering aspects. Astrologers vary in their opinion as to what the allowable orb should be, but virtually all astrologers agree that the smaller the ORB...the stronger the aspect!

ASPECTS:

ASPECTS deal with the RELATIONSHIP one PLANET has to another PLANET. Some aspects are considered to be EASY, while other aspects are considered to be CHALLENGING, or require ACTION. The MAJOR aspects are used by almost all astrologers and opinions on MINOR aspects vary. The MINOR aspects are not used by some astrologers, but other astrologers feel that the minor aspects are just as important as the major aspects. All astrologers agree about these aspects.

Some of these aspects are more difficult to identify and a computer program that will supply an **ASPECT GRID** to identify them for you can be quite helpful. In time...your eye will see the aspects without the use of an aspect grid. One does have to be careful and observe out-of-sign aspects as well.

	☉	☽	☿	♀	♂	♃	♄	♅	♆	♇
☉		□						✳		☍
☽			△							
☿										
♀		△								
♂						☌				
♃					☌					
♄										
♅	✳									
♆										
♇	☍									

30'

There are 360' DEGREES in a circle

EXERCISE: Draw lines from house cusp to house cusp that represent
30' 45' 60' 90' 120' 135' 150' 180' aspects in this wheel

It's Time to see what you Remember!

Place YOUR chart into this wheel and draw the ASPECT LINES for TRINES, SEXTILES, OPPOSITIONS & SQUARES!
HELPFUL HINT: USE RED Lines for the HARD aspects and BLUE Lines for the EASY ASPECTS!

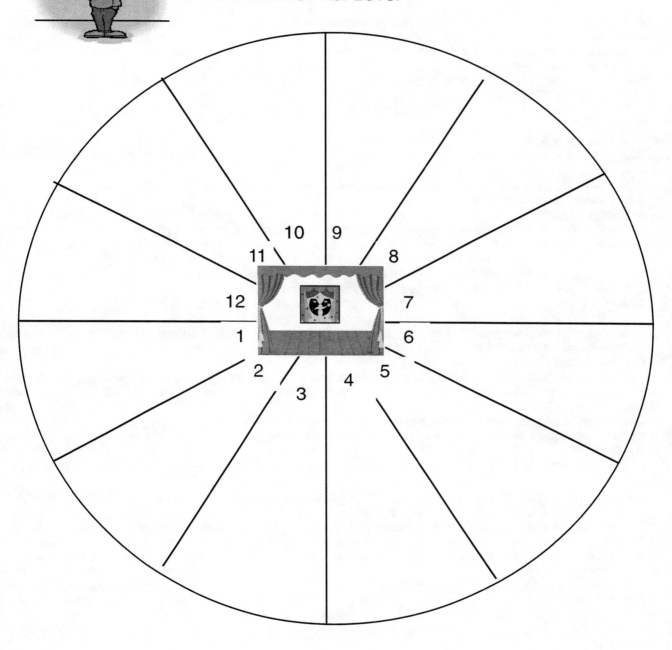

Astrological Glossary of Terms

Afflicted: Used to describe a planet which is unfavorably aspected; squares, oppositions and quincunxes. An ancient term which is still commonly used.

Air Signs: Gemini, Libra and Aquarius. Signs belonging to this Element represent the intellectual and thought process.

Anaretic degree: The final degree (29th degree) of any Sign. It is also known as the degree of fate.

Angles: The lines of the chart wheel which lie at 0 degrees (the ascendant), 90 degrees (the I.C.), 180 degrees (the descendant), and 270 degrees (the M.C.). These are major points in a chart and represent Cardinal Qualities.

Aquarian Age: A time period of 2000 years where the influence of Aquarius is prominent. An age lasts for 2000 years and moves backward through the Zodiac. The Age of Aquarius starts at approximately the new millennium.

Arc: An angular measurement between two celestial planets or points.

Ascendant: See Rising Sign

Aspects: The angular distance, calculated in specific number of degrees of the chart wheel, between two celestial planets or points. It also provides the nature of the relationship between planets.

Astrology: The study of the influence of celestial bodies on any behavior, activity or condition on Earth.

Birth Chart (also known as a Chart or Chart wheel): A 'map' detailing the positioning of the planets in the Signs at the specific moment of an individual's birth. The chart is rendered by using the individual's place, date and time of birth as the data source for this planetary snapshot.

Cardinal Signs: Aries, Cancer, Libra and Capricorn. This Quality represents initiative.

Celestial body: A physical form which exists in space; such as a planet.

Composite chart: Two individual charts which are merged to form one. It shows the relationship between the individuals whose charts are combined.

Configuration: An aspect involving three or more planets.

Conjunction: Two or more planets sitting next to each other within an acceptable orb, generally considered within 8 degrees for major aspects. A conjunction gives great strength to the energies of the interacting planets.

Constellation: A group of visible stars in the same section of the sky.

Cusp: The midway point between two Signs of the Zodiac; also used to refer to the start of a House within the chart wheel.

Cycle: A planet's Zodiacal period; the time it takes a planet or point to make one complete revolution in the heavens.

Decanate: The partitioning of each Sign into three equal parts of 10 degrees each. Each part is known as a decanate. Every Sign is composed of 30 degrees.

Declination: The arc of measurement in degrees north or south of the celestial equator.

Degree: A degree is 1/360 of a circle. In Astrology, degrees are the commonly-used unit of measurement.

Descendant: The opposite point from the ascendant; the cusp of the Seventh House. It describes one's interaction with another.

Earth Signs: Taurus, Virgo and Capricorn. Signs belonging to this Element represent a practical nature.

Eighth House: Also known as the House of Sex. It describes shared resources, inheritance, alimony, taxes and surgery. It is also the House of regeneration, death and rebirth.

Electional Astrology: The branch of Astrology which deals with selecting the best time to initiate any given activity or project.

Elements: A four-fold division of the Zodiac which is comprised of Fire, Earth, Air and Water. Signs of the same Element share similar characteristics. Also known as a Triplicity.

Eleventh House: Also known as the House of Friends. It describes friendships and acquaintances, as well as hopes and dreams. It rules groups, humanitarianism and philanthropic attitudes.

Ephemeris: An almanac which lists the Zodiacal positions of the Planets and other astronomical data for a given time period. Plural is ephemerides.

Equinox: Means a time of equal day and night. This occurs twice a year and marks the beginning of Spring and Autumn.

Feminine Signs: The Earth and Water Signs, comprised of Taurus, Cancer, Virgo, Scorpio, Capricorn and Pisces. Indicates passive and receptive energy.

Fifth House: Also known as the House of Pleasure. It describes romance, creativity, children, fun and speculation. It also rules the dramatic and one's artistic ability.

Fire Signs: Aries, Leo and Sagittarius. Signs belonging to this Element represent a fiery nature.

First House: Also known as the House of Self. It describes the outer personality. It is the image we project to the world, our mask.

Fixed Signs: Taurus, Leo, Scorpio and Aquarius. This Quality represents stubbornness and inflexibility.

Forecast: Plotting the movements of the planets to determine upcoming trends.

Fourth House: Also known as the House of Home. It describes the residence, real estate, ancestry and the past. It is also speaks to parental influence.

Grand Cross: A configuration in which four planets form mutual squares. It creates much tension.

Grand Trine: When three planets, generally of the same Element, meet each other to form a triangle. The energy of this configuration is harmonious.

Hard Aspect: Aspects which create tension and friction. Squares, oppositions and quincunxes are all hard aspects.

Horary Astrology: The branch of Astrology devoted to answering specific questions by means of a chart drawn up for the time the question is asked.

Horoscope: In this century, the word 'horoscope' has become synonymous with the daily 20-50 word predictions offered in newspapers, magazines and on the Internet. It literally means the 'marker of time,' and it is a map of the heavens at the time of one's birth (technically speaking, synonymous with 'birth chart').

Houses: The celestial sphere taken as a 360-degree circle divided into twelve sections. These sections are referred to by their numbers, such as 'the First House,' 'the Second House,' etc. Houses are generally numbered counterclockwise from the ascendant (starting at the nine o'clock position), with the House which begins at the ascendant known as 'the First House.' Each House speaks to a particular component of one's life.

I.C.: Immum Coeli. Latin for "bottom of the heavens". One of the four major angles of a birth chart; this one falls at the bottom of the chart wheel. It is the start of the Fourth House and is one of the most personal points of the chart.

Intercepted Sign or House: A House which appears within another House on the chart wheel. Common to those born in far northern or southern latitudes.

Jupiter: Represents luck, philosophy, religion, higher learning, ethical values, expansion, abundance and excesses. It also rules long distance travel, aspirations and judgment.

Karma Sign: Saturn is the Planet of Karma. Saturn is a strong disciplinarian and teaches us our lessons this lifetime. At times, this planet can be restricting and inhibiting. Joy is experienced once the lessons of Saturn have been learned. To understand your Karmic lesson, find what Sign Saturn was in at the time of your birth. This will reveal your Karmic Sign. Your Karma Sign is different from your Sun Sign or Star Sign!

Lights: An ancient term used for the Sun and the Moon.

Luck Sign: Jupiter is known as the Planet of Luck, particularly from ancient times. It rules your potential for growth and expansion on many levels -- physical, intellectual, spiritual and cultural. It also governs the accumulation of material assets, power and status. It describes your optimism and aspirations. Your Luck Sign is different from your Sun Sign or Star Sign!

M.C.: Medium Coeli. Latin word for "middle of the heavens". One of the four major angles of a birth chart, this one is at the top of the chart wheel. It is the start of the Tenth House, and it addresses public life and reputation.

Mars: Represents action, passion, drive and determinationpositions of the Planets and other astronomical data for a given time period. Plural is ephemerides.

Masculine Signs: Fire and Air Signs, comprised of Aries, Gemini, Leo, Libra, Sagittarius and Aquarius. It represents assertive and self-assured energy.

Mercury: Represents communication, intellect, consciousness, transportation, dexterity and the mind.

Modes: See "Qualities."

Moon: Represents the Mother and the women in one's life, nurturing, home, emotions, instinct and memory. It also represents one's emotional response to situations and experiences.

Mundane Astrology: The branch of Astrology which deals with places as opposed to people; world events and universal trends are the focal point.

Mutable Signs: Gemini, Virgo, Sagittarius and Pisces. This Quality represents a flexible nature.

Natal: Synonymous with 'birth.' Natal chart and birth chart are terms which can be used interchangeably.

Neptune: Rules music, television, movies, fashion, glamour, dreams, illusion, drugs, the intangible and the elusive. It also represents abstract thought, alcohol, the universal subconscious and the oceans of the Earth.

Ninth House: Also known as the House of Philosophy. It represents religion, travel, foreign countries, in-laws, higher education, publishing, import/export and ethics.

Opposition: When Planets are exactly opposite each other in the chart wheel; an arc of 180 degrees. Creates stress. Balance is needed in the presence of an opposition.

Orb: The space on the chart wheel measured in degrees, between planets and points, by which an aspect may vary from exactness and still remain effective. Out of Bounds: Planets which are outside the usual north or south measurement of the celestial equator within which planets rest.

Out-of-Sign: Also known as a dissociate aspect; addresses the importance of measuring aspects by degree rather than Sign. For example, a conjunction between a planet at 29 degrees Leo and 1 degree Virgo is within a 2 degree orb but not the same Sign. This weakens the aspect.

Planets: As used in Astrology, this refers to the Sun, Moon, Mercury, Venus, Mars, Jupiter, Saturn, Uranus, Neptune and Pluto. Earth is excluded, as it is our point of reference. In general, it is a major body which revolves around a Sun in a periodic orbit.

Pluto: Rules transformation, regeneration, rebirth, destruction, annihilation, power and elimination. It also represents atomic power, intensity, crime, death and the underworld.

Progressions: A method of advancing the planets and points of a natal chart to a particular time after birth. Used to illustrate one's evolution.

Qualities: The Signs are classified by their Qualities

Quincunx: An arc of 150 degrees. Also known as the inconjunct, this aspect creates a certain uneasiness and a feeling of discomfort, and it has karmic lessons to teach us. It is a minor aspect.

Report: An interpretation of one's birth chart. Also known as delineation.

Retrograde: When a planet appears to be traveling backwards from our perspective on Earth. The energy of a retrograde planet is less assertive and more internalized.

Rising Sign: Also known as the Ascendant. The degree at which the Zodiac rests over the eastern horizon of the birthplace at the moment of one's birth; commonly refers to the Sign which is peering over the horizon at that very moment. A new Sign rises approximately every two hours. The Rising Sign represents one's persona and image to the world.

Saturn: Represents discipline, responsibility, ambition, restriction, limitation and delays. It also rules older people, tradition, authority, structure, patience and wisdom through perseverance and age. It teaches us our lessons in life.

Second House: Also known as the House of Possessions. It describes your material assets, monetary income and the potential ways it may be earned. It also indicates what you value throughout life.

Secondary Progressions: See Progressions

Semi-Sextile: An arc of 30 degrees. This aspect creates unease; it is a minor aspect.

Seventh House: Also known as the House of Partnership. It represents marriage, joint partnerships, ventures and business partnerships. It also rules divorce, legalities, open confrontations, contracts, lawsuits and negotiations.

Sextile: An arc of 60 degrees; this is a favorable aspect. The planets involved are usually in compatible Elements. A sextile allows the influences of the planets to work in harmony; it brings forth opportunity.

Sun Sign: Originally referred to as your Star Sign, your Sun Sign represents the Sign of the Zodiac that the Sun was in at the time of your birth. The Sun rules will power and ego. It is the core of your potential and uniqueness as an individual; who you are and what you are about. Your Sun Sign represents the main direction and focus you want your life to take and your determination to accomplish what you set out to do. It represents your personal honesty and integrity, your ability to command respect and authority and your capacity to impress and influence others

Third House: Also known as the House of Communication. It is the way in which we express ourselves and think on an intellectual level. It also represents consciousness, siblings, neighbors and our local environment, as well as early education, mechanical dexterity and short trips.

Transit: The position and movement of a planet or point on any given day.

Trine: An arc of 120 degrees; the most harmonious aspect. In most cases, it joins planets in congenial Signs of the same Element. These energies combine with ease. The drawback, however, is the lack of challenge -- benefits are derived without effort.

Triplicity: See Elements

Twelfth House: Also known as the House of the Unconscious. It represents the hidden or unknown, the subconscious mind, the intangible, sleep, dreams, karma and spiritual debt. It rules solitude, confinement, fears, sorrow, secrets, hidden enemies, non-reality, institutions and charity.

Uranus: Represents the erratic, the bizarre, and the different. It rules freedom, inventions, originality, computers, technology, science, electricity, revolution, rebellion and change. Uranus breaks through barriers and tradition.

Venus: Represents love, romance, beauty, culture, the aesthetic, affection, one's social appeal and acceptability, good taste, harmony and values.

Void of course: A term describing a planet that does not make a major aspect before changing Signs. It is used primarily with respect to the Moon.

Water Signs: Cancer, Scorpio and Pisces. Signs belonging to this Element represent an emotional, sensitive and intuitive nature.

Zodiac: From the Greek word 'zodiakos,' literally meaning 'circle of animals.' A band in the heavens divided into twelve Signs, each containing 30 degrees of longitude and acting as the barometer for various human traits.

A Crossword Puzzle

ACROSS

2. There are _____ signs of the Zodiac.
4. The_____ sign in our chart represents our feelings.
6. The_____ in our solar system seem to exert an influence over our own electromagnetic energy fields.
7. Gemini, Libras & Aquarius are _____ signs.
8. Our _____ sign describes how our ego operates in our _____.
10. Aries, Leo & Sagittarius are _____ signs.
12. This is a _____. The north _____ is a point in the sky where the path of the sun and the moon cross and explains what we are trying to accomplish in this lifetime.
14. The _____ of influence between any two planets describes how close they are to each other.
16. People who have a lot of fire signs in their chart, are sometimes described as being _____.
20. The four _____ are known as Air, Fire, Earth & Water.
22. The _____moon tends to light up that area of our chart/life that needs to be addressed in any given month. There can be stress during this time. The _____ in our chart can be easy or difficult. (conjunctions, squares, trines oppositions)
24. The _____ signs tend to be strong-willed. They are Taurus, Leo, Scorpio & Aquarius.
26. The _____ signs tend to be leaders and are Aries, Cancer, Libra, Capricorn.

DOWN

2. The planet _____ describes our love nature and the things that we value.
3. _____ is called the planet of power & transformation.
4. _____ literally means "equal day & night".
5. There are _____ known "planets" that we use in astrology. Many more are being discovered! Water signs tend to be _____ and psychic.
6. The PLANETS describe the _____ that exist in our chart. The SIGNS show HOW the _____ work and the HOUSE show WHERE the _____ work.
8. The word _____ came from the word lunar or moon. The planet _____ is considered to be the planet of aggression and war.
10. Our _____ is what the sun sign in your _____chart represents.
11. This word is sometimes used instead of "Rising Sign".
12. The _____ signs tend to be practical, down to earth and are great at organizing! They also tend to be materialistic and require financial stability in their lives.
13. These terms: Cardinal, Fixed, Mutable, describe the _____ of the planets:
14. This planet has a 28 1/2 year cycle in your chart and describes the lessons you are here to experience. Once the lesson has been learned, you will receive your hard-earned rewards.
15. This element works well with the earth signs, and can produce a beautiful garden, a mud puddle or desert, depending on the amount of the mixture!

NOTES:

Chapter 5

It's time to take a look at your drama!…

Your CHART!

Let's take a look at your personal DRAMA!

Your personal STAR MAP™ or Astrology Chart shows where the planets were placed in the heavens at the exact hour of your birth. The PLANETS in a chart represent certain ENERGIES, the SIGN those PLANETS are in, show HOW the ENERGY is used, and the HOUSES the PLANETS fall in, show WHERE, or in what area of your life you will USE those energies. Everything is energy. We are electromagnetic, MULTI-DIMENSIONAL, spiritual beings inhabiting a physical body. Interpretation of your chart is based upon analyzing the archetypal symbols for the human condition. No one's chart is all "good" or all "bad". One can use the energies in a mature or immature way. "Difficult" aspects can represent challenges, as well as strengths a person might have, while "easy" aspects can represent certain talents you were born with.

Your "STAR MAP" is your blueprint for being and shows the many CYCLES of expression that you will experience on this EARTH SCHOOL planet. Understanding your astrology chart is a most effective way to "conscious awareness" and engages that part of you that already knows everything. It is very revealing, empowering, quite exciting...and a lot of FUN!

Your Astrology Chart is your SCRIPT, and represents the many ROLES you play in life. Like an ACTOR, you are not always on stage, you may find yourself changing costumes, studying your lines, or just waiting for your entrance. When the play is over...you will take a bow and await your REVUE!

Congratulations! Now that you are familiar with the terminology...you are ready to analyze your own chart!

86

My CHART

My chart shows that I have (# of PLANETS)

- I have _____ Planets in CARDINAL signs,
- I have _____ Planets in FIXED signs
- I have _____ Planets in MUTABLE signs.

- I have _____ Planets in AIR signs
- I have _____ Planets in FIRE signs
- I have _____ Planets in EARTH signs
- I have _____ Planets in WATER signs

The Sun is the life-giving heart of our solar system and rules will and individuality. It is the core of your potential and uniqueness as an individual: who you are and what you are about. It represents the main direction and focus you want your life to take and your determination to accomplish what you set out to do. The Sun's position in your horoscope demonstrates the depth of your personal honesty and integrity, the ability to command respect and authority, to impress and influence others. It indicates the stamp of your character, the deepest flavor of your individuality.

My SUN sign is _____. The symbol for my sun sign is _____.
The Sun's influence in my chart represents my *basic personality and my ego needs*.
Other key words for the Sun's influence are
_____
_____.
My Sun sign in _____ is ruled by the PLANET_____, which deals with
_____. I could say this
about myself, that as a Sun in _____, I tend to be
_____
 My Sun in _____ resides in the _____HOUSE of my chart. This
house rules_____.
This would indicate that my ego needs are most satisfied when

_____
_____
_____
_____
_____

The MOON reflects the power of the inner light, channeling and molding it into the shape of your personality. While the Sun stands for the character, or ego-self, the Moon displays your nature in a way that can be grasped by the outer world. Ruling desire as opposed to self, or need as opposed to reason, it indicates your feelings about yourself; how you handle relationships and your automatic emotional response to situations and experiences. The MOON is based upon past life experiences. The MOON manages the flow of your daily functions: physical, emotional and mental. The MOON symbolizes your home base and domestic environment, it represents babies and young children, your mother and other important women in your life.

My MOON sign is _____. The symbol for my MOON sign is _____. The MOON's influence in my chart represents my automatic emotional response to life and my emotional needs. Other key words for the MOON's influence are :

My MOON in _____ is ruled by the PLANET_____, which deals with _____. I could say this about myself, that as a MOON in _____, I tend to be _____ when it comes to emotional responses. My MOON in _____ resides in the _____ HOUSE of my chart. This house rules matters dealing with _____.

This would indicate that my emotional needs are most satisfied when

_____
_____.

MERCURY symbolizes mentality: your intellect and mental outlook, the way you think and communicate. MERCURY, as Hermes, is the emblem for the magus, the wise counselor, divine messenger -- and prince of thieves! This fast-moving planet stands for ideas, methods and information, especially as expressed through communication and media. MERCURY indicates your manual dexterity and mechanical skills and also governs transportation: how you get where you're going, both physically and mentally. Are you a hare, or a tortoise? MERCURY's position in your chart will tell all!

The PLANET MERCURY was in the sign of _____ when I was born. The symbol for MERCURY is _____ . MERCURY's influence in my chart represents how my mind operates and how I think. My MERCURY in _____ is ruled by the PLANET_____, which deals with _____.
I could say this about myself, that as a MERCURY in _____, when it comes to intellectual ability. I tend to be_____.
My MERCURY in _____ resides in the _____ HOUSE of my chart. This house rules _____.
This would indicate that my INTELLECTUAL needs are most satisfied when

_____
_____
_____.

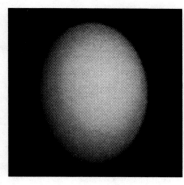

VENUS was the Goddess of love. In your chart she represents the good things in life: money, pleasure, romance & artistic endeavors as well as female relationships and social interactions at every level. VENUS rules your social attitudes and behavior, along with your aesthetic tastes and inclinations. VENUS represents the things you value in life, as well as the principles of harmony and equilibrium. Her placement describes your inclination toward romance, marriage and other partnerships, your capacity for artistic abilities, for humor, and the pursuit of pleasure.

From a romantic point of view, VENUS in a man's chart shows the kinds of women most likely to desired, while her placement in a woman's chart indicates the ways in which the subject is likely to present herself to attract the interest of romantic partners. VENUS rules desire in all its forms. VENUS also governs the flow of money and the financial conditions in your life. In ancient mythology, VENUS, the beautiful love goddess, was always getting up to something with Mars, the fierce god of war. None of the other gods could ever figure out what the lovely VENUS saw in the headstrong, arrogant Mars, but she certainly fancied him, no matter what anyone else said or thought.

The PLANET VENUS was in the sign of _____ when I was born. The symbol for MERCURY is _____. VENUS influences in my chart represent my needs for pleasure, creativity and love. Other key words for VENUS are

My VENUS in _____is ruled by the PLANET_____, which deals with _____. I could say this about myself, that VENUS in _____, tends to express itself _____ when it comes to my romantic needs. My Venus in _____ resides in the _____ HOUSE of my chart. This house rules
_____.

This would indicate that my romantic needs are most satisfied when
_____
_____
_____
_____.

MARS, the god of warriors, rules physical energy and efforts. His placement in your chart expresses the strength and direction of the physical force that drives your ego. MARS fires your emotions, but also powers your mental endeavors and communicative skills. The red planet governs energy, strength, courage, life-force and expansion. MARS describes male relationships and associations, risk-taking inclinations, and the physical challenges you are likely to encounter. When MARS is well-placed, it endows powerful energy and an indomitable will to succeed, but when it is poorly placed, it can mean accidents, injuries or other forms of violence, according to the inclinations of the sign and house concerned.

MARS rules my needs for self-expression, aggression, desire & anger. From a romantic point of view, MARS in a woman's chart shows the most desired kinds of men, while his placement in a man's chart indicates the activities or mode of action undertaken in pursuit of romantic inclinations and desires. Other key words for MARS are:

The PLANET MARS was in the sign of _____ when I was born. The symbol for MARS is _____. The MARS influences in my chart represent _____

My MARS in the sign of _____ and it is ruled by the PLANET _____, which deals with _____. I could say this about myself, that when it comes to what I desire, MARS in _____, tends to express it- self _____ .
My MARS in _____ resides in the _____HOUSE of my chart. This house rules

_____.
This would indicate that my desire needs are most satisfied when

_____
_____
_____
_____.

 In ancient mythology, JUPITER was considered to be the King of the Gods. He ruled over everything. JUPITER rules the potential for growth and expansion on many levels: physical, intellectual, spiritual, cultural, and the accumulation of material assets, power and status. Jupiter describes your optimism and aspirations. JUPITER is a giant self-illuminating planet, radiating more energy than it receives, in keep- ing with his role as lord and teacher of the gods. Traditionally de- scribed as the greater fortune, JUPITER governs optimism, joy, luck and well being. When well aspected, he provides superb opportunities for expansion and success. Poorly aspected, he generates over-confidence and foolhardy actions with little care for the consequences. JUPITER spends about a year in each sign, taking twelve years to complete the journey through all twelve signs.

The PLANET JUPITER was in the sign of_____ when I was born. The symbol for JUPITER is_____.

JUPITER influences in my chart are considered to be LUCKY and represent my needs for expansion, vision, and travel. Other key words for JUPITER are:

My JUPITER in _____is ruled by the PLANET_____, which deals with

_____.

I could say this about myself, that when it comes to good fortune and how I will most grow through experience , JUPITER in the sign of _____, tends to express itself

_____ .

My JUPITER   resides in the _____HOUSE of my chart. This house rules

_____.

This would indicate that my expansiveness, optimism and good fortune will be seen

_____

_____

_____.

SATURN, sometimes known as "father time" or "the grim reaper", rules the responsibilities, restrictions and limitations we are apt to encounter, and the lessons we must learn in life. He does not deny or diminish imagination, inspiration, spirituality, or good fortune, but he does demand that you work for them and that these things be given structure and meaning. The karmic lessons we have come to experience and overcome in this lifetime are expressed by SATURN. He spends around two and a half years in each sign, taking about twenty-nine years on his journey through all the signs, at which time we will experience what is known as our SATURN Return which presents us with the challenge to rise to new levels of awareness, or face the consequences of having failed to gain the wisdom required so to do. When Saturn in the heavens returns to the zodiacal degree where he was placed in your birth chart, you are said to be experiencing your *Saturn Return*. This only happens once every 29 years, so at around age 28-30, 57-59 (and if you live long enough) 86-88 you have what astrologers call a Saturn Return. This signifies a time of transition, from one life-phase to the next. The first Saturn return (around age 28-30) marks the transition from the Phase of Youth to the Phase of Maturity; the second from the Phase of Maturity to the Phase of Wisdom. The last one, if reached, seems usually to mark the transition either to the next world or else back to a second childhood! As the SATRUN Return approaches, often our lives seem to speed up, as if hurrying to clear out old baggage from the past, to lighten the load for the next stage. Important things that either finalize old issues, or prepare the ground for new developments tend to occur with increasing frequency. Relationships and major life-decisions are often the focal points for this clearing out of karmic baggage.

The PLANET SATURN was in the sign of _____ when I was born. The symbol for SATURN is _____. SATURN   influences in my chart represent my needs for structure, order and responsibility. Other key words for SATURN are

My SATURN in _____ is ruled by the PLANET_____,
which deals with _____.
I could say this about myself, that SATURN in _____, tends to express itself _____
when it comes to what I desire. My SATURN in _____ resides in the
_____ HOUSE of my chart. This house rules

_____.

This would indicate that I could find difficulty in and my lessons in life appear to be

_____

_____

_____.

URANUS, the planet of sudden and unexpected changes, rules freedom and originality. In society it rules radical ideas and people, as well as revolutionary events that upset established structures. and among all planets, it most governs genius. The personal implications of URANUS in your life are shown by its house position and its aspects with other planets in your chart. It describes areas of unpredictability and difference. Being highly unorthodox, URANUS identifies the unusual or unique. Friends and associations to which you belong are indicated, as well as your potential involvement with arcane studies, science and technology, computers, and the media.

URANUS, one of the outer, transpersonal planets, takes around seven years to transit one sign, or about 84 years to move through all twelve signs. Groups of people with URANUS in the same sign are separated by 84 years, so the influence of this planet is primarily generational. The Industrial Revolution, the American and French Revolutions and our current Computer Age most represent this energy.

The PLANET URANUS was in the sign of _____ when I was born. The
symbol for URANUS is _____. URANUS influences in my chart represent
my needs for being unique, change and variety. Other key words for URANUS are

My URANUS in _____ is ruled by the PLANET _____,
which deals with _____.
I could say this about myself, that when it comes to what I most need in the way of freedom
of expression, URANUS in _____, tends to express itself

_____
My URANUS in _____ resides in the _____ HOUSE of my chart.
This house rules _____
_____. This would indicate that my needs to
express myself originally and freely are most satisfied when

_____

_____

_____.

NEPTUNE was the God of the oceans and the seas. In our chart it is seen as the planet of deception as well as spiritual enlightenment, it rules the oppressed and abandoned, the misfits of society. On a higher level it rules visionaries, and those who are glamorous and charismatic. It represents love on a humanitarian plane, spirituality, mysticism, and ideals.

Speaking personally, NEPTUNE's house position and its aspects with other planets in your chart will describe spirituality, abstract thinking, illusion, disillusionment, and areas of your life where things aren't always what they seem. It rules derangement, guilt, persecution and describes the potential for experiences related to confinement, abandonment, and addiction or physical intolerance to drugs and alcohol.

NEPTUNE is one of the outer, transpersonal planets, and it spends about thirteen years in each sign, taking around 164 years to move through all twelve signs. Since 164 years separate people born during its transit of one sign and those born when it returns, Neptune's significance in any sign is described as generational or historical.

The PLANET NEPTUNE was in the sign of _____ when I was born. The symbol for NEPTUNE is _____. NEPTUNE influences in my chart represent idealism and my needs for love on a more spiritual plane, fantasy & illusion. Other key words for NEPTUNE are

My NEPTUNE in _____ is ruled by the PLANET_____, which deals with _____. I could say this about myself, that NEPTUNE in _____, tends to express itself _____ when it comes to my fantasies & illusions. My NEPTUNE in _____ resides in the _____ HOUSE of my chart. This house rules

_____.
This would indicate that my needs for idealism are most satisfied when

_____
_____
_____.

PLUTO, was known as the lord of the underworld, and in the chart, this planet symbolizes the forces of deep transformation in our lives. A slow-moving planet, PLUTO's influence is in general most clearly noticeable as it distinguishes one generation from the next. In your personal life, PLUTO's significance is found in its house position and the aspects it makes to other planets in your chart. Pluto rules intense energy, signifying the areas in which you consciously or subconsciously seek to exercise power or control. PLUTO, linked to your karmic responsibility, also indicates those areas where you need to gain the deepest level of understanding.

PLUTO is the outermost known planet in our system, and it takes around 248 years to complete its journey through all twelve signs of the zodiac . The period PLUTO spends in each sign can vary from twelve years to thirty-two years, due to the eccentricity of its orbit.

The PLANET PLUTO was in the sign of _____ when I was born. The symbol for NEPTUNE is _____. PLUTO influences in my chart represent my needs for complete transformation, power & seeing into the depth of matters. Other key words for PLUTO are

My PLUTO in _____is ruled by the PLANET_____, which deals with _____.
I could say this about myself, that PLUTO in _____, tends to express itself _____ when it comes to what I find powerful. My PLUTO in _____ resides in the _____ HOUSE of my chart. This house rules _____.
This would indicate that my needs for power and to transform are most satisfied when _____
_____

My Ascendant or RISING SIGN is:_____
I tend to see the world_____
Others tend to see me as:_____
_____.

☊   My NORTH NODE is in the sign of _____. It is in my _____HOUSE. This tells me that my path or goals in life are to

_____
_____.

☋   My SOUTH NODE is in the sign of _____. It is in the _____ HOUSE. This tells me that I am trying to leave behind my need for (to)

_____
_____.

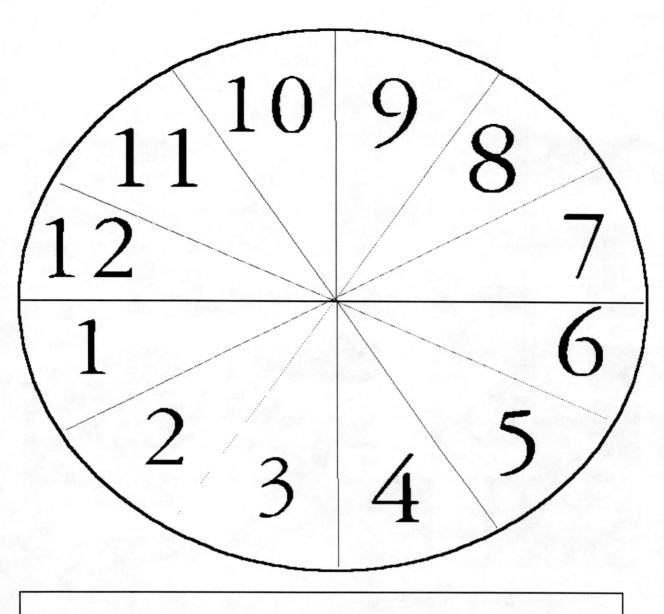

FOR_____

BIRTHDATE_____TIME_____AM_____PM

PLACE_____

Ascendant_____   Jupiter_____

Sun_____   Saturn_____

Moon_____   Uranus_____

Mercury_____   Neptune_____

Venus_____   Pluto_____

Mars_____   Chiron_____

North Node_____   South Node_____

AIR_____   FIRE_____   EARTH_____   WATER_____

CARDINAL_____   FIXED_____   MUTABLE_____   M_____   F_____

Kathleen Scott, C.A.P.
www.No1Starwoman.com   no1starwoman@juno.com

The Answers to your Crossword Puzzle

	1	2	3	4	5	6	7	8	9	10	11	12	13	14
2					T	W	E	L	V	E				S
3					E			U		G				A
4		M	O	O	N			N		O				T
5						E		A				E		U
6			P	L	A	N	E	T	S			A	I	R
7			L			E		I				R		N
8		S	U	N		R		C	H	A	R	T		
9			T			G			S			H	O	W
10			O		F	I	R	E		T				A
11						E				R				T
12				T	E	S	T		N	O	D	E		E
13					M					L				R
14					O					O	R	B		
15					T			M		G				
16		V	I	S	I	O	N	A	R	Y				
17		E			O			R					Q	
18		N			N			S					U	
19		U			A						A		A	
20		S		E	L	E	M	E	N	T	S		L	
21				Q							C		I	
22			F	U	L	L		A	S	P	E	C	T	S
23				I							N		Y	
24				N			F	I	X	E	D			
25				O							A			
26				X		C	A	R	D	I	N	A	L	
27											T			

STAR MAP Reports™

Basic NATAL Chart & STAR MAP Report. Your NATAL chart is your SCRIPT (no one else has the same script), and is based upon the exact TIME, PLACE & DATE of your birth. Your SCRIPT shows the many ROLES you will play on the great stage called life. There seems to be many dimensions to what is called your "personality" (mental, emotional, physical & spiritual "selves" within yourself!), the ROLE/ROLES you are playing. Knowing your chart (your SCRIPT) can help you with TIMING in life and assist you in making more CONSCIOUS CHOICES in your life. **($25)**

The **COSMIC CUPID STAR MAP Reports™ ROMANCE Reports for Lovers** include Individual Profile Reports which describe the relationship potential of each person (2) + Romantic Interpretation, which includes how the two people experience each other as well as the relationship from the perspective of each person. **($45.00)**

The **CHART SYNASTRY or CHART COMPARISON Reports**, used **for family or friendship**, include Individual Profile reports (2) + Synastry or Chart Comparison. (2 different ways of viewing a relationship potential). This report discovers the most significant issues of the relationship and emphasizes these issues! A forecast for the relationship is also included. These reports are each approximately 10-15 pages in length. **($45.00)**

The **BUSINESS RELATIONSHIP STAR MAP Report** can tell how you and your partner (s) will interact with each other. It analyzes your strengths and weaknesses individually as well as a partnership. This report also gives future trends for people engaged in running or making business decisions. Each report is 7-12 pages long for a 3 month period. **TOTAL: $50.00 for 2 people. $75.00 for 3 people. $100.00 for 4 people**.

The **BABY STAR MAP Report** is written specifically for parents and it focuses on issues that parents are concerned about for their baby: the needs, talents, potential problems, health, relationship to parents, the school environment, etc. This is a MUST for parents! It makes an excellent GIFT for the new parents! Each report is about 12-14 pages in length. **($25.00)**

The **CHILD STAR MAP Report** is written specifically for parents and it focuses on issues that parents are concerned about for their children: the needs, talents, potential problems, health, relationship to parents, the school environment, etc. This is a MUST for parents! It makes an excellent GIFT for the new parents! The report provides the positions of the planets at the time of birth. Then as each chapter begins, the astrological influence is noted. The report is written without jargon and is easy to understand. Each report is approximately 15-18 pages. **($25.00)**

FORECAST REPORTS

The **PROGRESSED STAR MAP Report** describes what is currently happening within yourself on a psychological level of growth and awareness. This report is usually done at the time of your birthday each year and is based upon the day-for-a-year premise. The report is 7-12 pages long. Cost **$15.00** per Report.

Your Personal FUTURE FORECASTS/TRANSITS STAR MAP Report describes the outside circumstances which can be influencing you. This report can cover several days, months or years and will give you a DAILY interpretation which is uniquely yours! The length of a one-month forecast is approximately 25-30 pages long. **$15.00 per month. $130 for the year ahead!**

LIFE PATH & Major THEMES Report blends psychological, spiritual and material potentials found in each individual. This is a surprisingly comprehensive and insightful report! Each report is about 10-13 pages in length. **($20.00)**

The **KARMA Report** will tell you what the planets and their aspects say about your personal karma! One of your Karmic indicators is the Nodes of the Moon in your Astrological Chart. Your individual chart will tell you about your South Node, symbolizing lessons from past lives, and your North Node, which shows your potential. Your Karmic task is to evolve from your South Node and head toward your North Node. It is your choice to cast off whatever is holding you back from a past life and fly toward the future. Your Karma Report offers you information on your 12th House, Saturn and Jupiter. These astrological elements tell you about your most important past life experiences and offer a guide to your Karmic gifts. Each chapter of this report includes your personal Karmic lesson. ($25.00)

The **TEEN FORECAST** Report which is written specifically for **TEENS and young people up to 24 years!** It is unique in that it focuses on issues that are important to this age group. It is written in modern language for modern times for today's young people who are crossing the bridge from childhood to adulthood in today's fast-paced and quickly changing times. The approximate report length is about 10-12 pages/month! **($15/month $130/year).**

Use the form below to fill out your personal profile so that I may create your NATAL CHART or STAR MAP Reports.

CALL: 949.723.0030   **Mail your checks to:**
Kathleen Scott   217 Tremont Drive Newport Beach, CA 92660
For CREDIT CARD purchases:
You may also go to my website for further ORDERING information.
no1starwoman@juno.com   www.no1starwoman.com

Your NAME:_____

Address:_____

TEL:_____CELL:_____

E-Mail:_____

For EACH Person's CHART or REPORT PLEASE INCLUDE:

NAME:_____
BIRTH DATE: _____BIRTH TIME :_____AM _____PM

BIRTHPLACE:_____
　　　　　　　　City　　　　　　　　　　　State　　　　　Country

Each Star Map Report™ is approximately 12-25 pages in length

❑ NATAL CHART Only		FREE!
❑ NATAL CHART & STAR MAP Report		$25
❑ CHILD STAR MAP Report		$25
❑ COSMIC CUPID ROMANCE Report (2 people)		$45
❑ Chart SYNASTRY/Chart COMPARISON Report:		$45
❑ BUSINESS RELATIONSHIP STAR MAP Report (per person)		$25
❑ PROGRESSED Star Map Report		$15
❑ FUTURE FORECAST /TRANSITS STAR MAP Report		
	$15/Month	$130/Year
❑ KARMA Report		$25
❑ LIFE PATH & MAJOR THEMES Report		$20
❑ TEEN Forecast	$15/Month	$130/Year
❑ TOTAL + S & H (ADD $3.95)_____		

☐ Additional **Self-Discovery Workbook in Astrology for BEGINNERS**
☐ Additional **Self-Discovery Workbook in Astrology for TEENS**
☐ Additional **INTERMEDIATE Self-Discovery Workbook in Astrology**
☐ Additional **ADVANCED Self-Discovery Workbook in Astrology**
　　　Be sure to Specify which LEVEL Books you wish to order

☐ 1-9 Copies $20 Each + S&H　　☐ 10 + Copies $15 Each + S&H

Kathleen Scott, C.A.P.

No1Starwoman.com

"All the World's a Stage…"
Know Your Chart...You'll Know Your Part!"

Kathleen Scott is a Certified Astrological Professional, ISAR, The International Society for Astrological Research, and has successfully counseled, taught and lectured on Astrology since 1976 in Mexico, France, Canada & England. She was a featured Astrologer for CLUB MED and MAGIC ISLAND, in Newport Beach, CA and her credentials include having successfully completed the course "Harmonics in Astrology" at Girton College, Cambridge, England under John Addey & Charles Harvey. She is an active member of SCAN, the Southern California Astrological Network. Kathleen's many free-lance articles on Astrology have appeared in national women's magazines as well as her Astrology advice column, **"Your Rising Sign"**, for local newspapers. Her current monthly column **"COSMIC Patterns"** can be viewed on **www.no1starwoman.com.**

www.cosmiconnections.com & **www.anewday-anewway.com,** were created to support and promote metaphysical subjects, writers, teachers, coaches, classes, workshops, movies, cable TV & TV programming of higher consciousness. If you are particular and are looking for the right romantic partner, you can go to **www.cosmic-cupid.com,** a matchmaking directory website for the most particular.

As a spiritually focused Astrologer, Kathleen specializes in helping you find your true purpose in life, and can assist you in relationship & career counseling, as well as determining the best timing for those important life decisions, using the ancient science of Astrology. Kathleen lives live in southern California. Besides teaching & counseling clients, she is also available for lecturing, workshops & parties.

What Kathleen's clients have to say....

"That was the first reading I've ever had, and any creeping scepticism has been washed away. That was really an impressive consultation - thanks so much No1Starwoman!"
"She was great! I felt as if I had known her my entire life. I plan to call again when I have other questions".
"This is the first time I have ever done anything like this. The Natal Chart & Report summed up my personality to a tee. It also helped me to look at areas that I need to improve in. Thank you "
"She was great, and very helpful with timing on my career and relationship questions. Thank you! I give her a 5 star recommendation :-) Be confident that she will give you the help you need. "
"Really great information! Easy to talk to and understand. Will call again. "
"I enjoyed talking with you. You have given me a lot to think about. I wasn't real sure about astrology. I never really trusted that the person giving the advice was into it for the right reason. You seem to enjoy your work and that is always a good sign that a person is in it for all the right reasons. Thanks again. "
"Kathy is WONDERFUL and knows her stuff...Love her sense of humor too...Thanks again."